Where do I Belong?

Where do I Belong?

From Kabul to London –
A Refugee's Life

NEW REVISED EDITION

Shabibi Shah

Longstone

LONDON

First published in 2001 by Shabibi Shah

Second edition in 2008 by
Longstone Books
33 Theatre Street
London SW11 5ND

ISBN 978-0-9554373-5-9

Memoirs series editor: Mary Simpson
Cover design by Andrew Corbett
Designed and set by Long House Publishing Services, Cumbria
Printed and bound by CPI Anthony Rowe, Chippenham, Wiltshire

Copies can be ordered from Shabibi Shah
43A Haling Road
South Croydon
Surrey CR2 6HS
shabibishah@yahoo.com

To my dear Zafar,
who did not live long enough
to return to his beautiful homeland

To my people,
who suffered and died from the invasion and civil
war

To my dearest children, Yama, Parissa and
Sulaiman,
who are worth living for

Preface to the second edition

It is seven years now since I published the first edition of my book. My original reason for writing a book about my life was simply to improve my English and escape from the pain and loneliness after the death of my dear husband, Zafar. As the book progressed, I began to see how it could help my three children to learn about the country they originally came from and which I still love.

I was really surprised when the first edition sold out. I was also touched to receive letters from people I had never met saying how much they had enjoyed the book. One person said the book had opened her eyes to the fact that not all refugees come from poor backgrounds and have limited education. Another said it had helped her to understand the background to the violence of present-day Afghanistan. Many people were disappointed that they could no longer buy a copy of the book, so I decided rather than just reprinting the original to use the opportunity to bring it up-to-date.

So as I revised the book and also talked to my children, I found I was able to add some new memories and correct some inaccuracies in the first edition. I realise how important it is today to understand some of the history of Afghanistan, especially for Afghan children who are now settled in different parts of the world, so I have added some more detail to explain the background to the invasion by Russia and the rise of the Taliban. I have also added a final chapter bringing the book up-to-date, describing my life in England after Zafar's death and my return visit to Afghanistan in 2004.

When I started writing my book, the communists were still in power in Afghanistan and I did not feel I could be as frank as I can now about who was to blame for Zafar's imprisonment. Ten years on, the political situation has changed and I am able to write more honestly.

I have published poetry in my first language, Dari. Since I have been in England I have also written a number of poems in English as a way of expressing my feelings. Although I know these poems are not very sophisticated, they do give a flavour of the emotions that are an essential part of my story, so I have included one of these at the start of each chapter.

Acknowledgements

It is not easy writing in a second language and I am grateful for all the help and support I have received both for the first edition and for this revised second edition.

I would like to thank Janis Say who encouraged me to keep on writing and patiently read and re-read the manuscript of the first edition. Thanks also to Catherine Dory who typed the manuscript, to Linda Elder the editor, and to Elizabeth Harland, Ralph Russell, Marion Molteno and Dr Sayed A. Mousavi who read and commented on the first draft. My son Sulaiman gave me invaluable help in writing my story, although I know he found it boring to correct my spelling and poor English. I am particularly grateful to Stella Weaver, whose generosity made it possible for me to publish the first edition.

I would not have been able to complete this revised edition of my book without the help of Mary Simpson, who patiently discussed the revisions chapter by chapter, suggested improvements and polished my imperfect English. I would also like to thank Ralph Russell and Carole Fries for their helpful comments and corrections. Finally thanks to all those involved with Longstone books, who made it possible for me to publish this second edition.

Shabibi Shah
May 2008

Time line for the main events in the book

Political	For Shabibi and family
1933 King Zahir Shah comes to to the throne	1947 Shabibi born
	1964 Shabibi goes to university
	1966 Shabibi engaged to Zafar
	1967 Shabibi married Zafar
	1968 Son Yama born
	1971 Shabibi, Zafar and Yama go on holiday to America via Russia
	1972 daughter Parissa born
1973 Former Prime Minister Mohammed Davoud seizes power. End of monarchy, start of Russian influence	1973–1976 Zafar student in America, Shabibi in Kabul teaching
	1976 Zafar returns to Kabul, works as independent journalist for *Caravan* newspaper
1978 Communists come to power under Taraki	1978 Zafar works for Libyan Embassy
September 1979 Deputy Prime Minister Amin kills Taraki, seizes power	
Dec 1979 Soviet troops, invade Afghanistan, overthrow Amin, Communist government under Babrak Karmal	

1979–1986 Communist
government under Babrak Karmal

1986 Mohammed Najibullah
elected President, new
constitution
1989 Withdrawal of Soviet troops
1990—1996 Civil war between
warlords, Mujahideen, Taliban

1996—2002 Taliban in power
11 September 2001 Attacks on
the USA
2002 Americans / Mujahideen
overthrow the Taliban
2004 Hamid Karzai becomes
President of new government,
civil war continues

1980 Zafar in prison first time
1981 Zafar works for Palestinian
Embassy, Zafar in prison second
time
1982 Son Sulaiman born
6 March 1983 Zafar leaves
Afghanistan
21 March 1983 Shabibi and children
leave Afghanistan
1984 Arrive in England, move to
Verrals
1985 Move to Croydon, Zafar's first
stroke

1992 Yama marries Surrita
1992 Murder of Ruhullah
1993 Death of Zafar

2004 Shabibi and Parissa return to
Afghanistan

Map of Afghanistan

Source: www.appliedlanguage.com/maps_of_the_world

Chapter One
My early years in Afghanistan

A bridge had collapsed
behind me
All washed out
No way to cross over
Cut off from people who
matter to me
Here are bits of me that cannot fit
into a new pattern
I hold on to the memory
It links me to the other side
of the river
I hold tight to it
Like a child who treasures
her doll

I was born in Kabul, the capital of Afghanistan, in 1947. Afghanistan lies in the heart of Asia providing a crossroads between East and West. It is surrounded by Iran in the west, Pakistan in the south and east, China in the north-east, and Tajikistan, Turkmenistan and Uzbekistan in the north. The climate is dry and there are many mountains and deserts, with some plains in the north and south-west.

The friendly and hospitable people are a mixture of over fifty scattered ethnic groups who have conquered the mountains and deserts. The largest groups are Pashtun, Tajik, Hazara, Uzbek and Aimaq. The official languages are Dari (Dari is the version of Farsi that is spoken in Afghanistan) and Pashto but there are also a number of minority languages spoken.

The Afghan people are fiercely proud of their culture and history. The country has been invaded by many different countries including the Greeks under Alexander the Great, the Mongols under Genghis Khan, the British and the Russians, but none succeeded in fully conquering the Afghani people. King Ahmad Shah Durrani, who extended his rule beyond present-day Afghanistan to Pakistan, Iran and India in the eighteenth century, has been called the founder of modern Afghanistan. Much of this large kingdom was ceded to the British in the nineteenth century and it was not until 1919 that Afghanistan regained independence. From 1933 to 1973 the country was ruled by King Zahir Shah, and it was during his reign, in 1947, that I was born in Kabul.

The main religion is Islam which was introduced into Afghanistan in the eighth century and has provided a unifying factor between the different ethnic groups. There are also small groups of Hindus and Sikhs and a few members of the Jewish community.

There are two main sects of Islam, Sunni and Shia. The division between the two goes right back to the history of our faith. When the Prophet Mohammed died in AD 632 his close friend and faithful follower, Abu Bakr Siddiq, became the first Caliph of Islam but died two years later. The second Caliph, Omar, served for ten years and was renowned for his fairness, but was then stabbed to death by a slave while conducting prayers. On his death bed he selected a small trustworthy group to choose a leader. Osman was elected and served for eleven years before being tragically murdered. Ali, the Prophet Mohammed's cousin and son-in-law, became the fourth Caliph, but Muawiya, who was from Caliph Osman's clan, blamed Ali for not seeking out Osman's murderers. War followed and Muawiya seized the leadership from Ali but Ali's followers refused to accept Muawiya as leader.

From this point onwards Islam was split into two groups: the followers of Ali were called Shias and the followers of Muawiya, Sunni. With the appointment of Muawiya, the democratic society desired by the Prophet Mohammed changed to one of aristocracy. Muawiya nominated his son Yazid, who is always described as an atrocious, cold-hearted person, to succeed him on his death. When Yazid came to power, Ali's son and the Prophet Mohammed's grandson Husein, a man of peace, stood by his principles and refused to accept such a man as leader.

Husein and seventy-two of his family and followers were then massacred in one day in the desert of Karbala, and only one young boy survived, Ali ibn al Husein. Since then Karbala, a city in Iraq where Husein and his family are buried, is a holy place for all Shia Muslims. This massacre was the most outrageous event in Muslim political history.

The majority of Muslims in Afghanistan are Sunnis but my family were from the minority Shias, and my father claimed to be a direct descendant of the Prophet Mohammed through Ali ibn al Husein. People who are descendants of Prophet Mohammed are called Sayeds. At the beginning of the fifteenth century my Shia Sayed ancestors migrated from what is now Iran to Khorasan, the name for Afghanistan until the nineteenth century. They settled around Bamiyan province in Central Afghanistan, where they were welcomed by the Hazara people, a minority group who were also Shias. The Hazaras gave shelter and land to the Sayeds and accepted them as religious leaders. The grave of my great-grandfather, Sayed Shah Qubad, is still worshipped as a shrine in that area. My father was also greatly respected as a Sayed and I remember that at the Muslim festival, Eid, people would come to pay their respects to him, and they would kiss the hands and touch the eyes of both my father and all his children. I always felt privileged and important that even old men with long flowing beards would show us such respect.

Shia communities, both in Afghanistan and other Muslim countries, always commemorate the anniversary of Husein's massacre by gathering together to mourn. During that month we do not listen to music, wear new and colourful clothes or get married. As a child I knew nothing of the conflict between Shia and Sunni and just enjoyed the excitement of the gatherings. When I grew older and understood the conflict I still referred to myself as 'just a Muslim', refusing to align myself with either sect despite my father's strictness, although I never forgave the barbaric behaviour of Yazid towards my ancestor. A friend much later asked to which sect I belonged and to her surprise my answer was to none and both.

'Everyone has to have a basic root,' she said.

'We damaged Islam enough by separation. My root is Islam and my ancestor is the Prophet Mohammed,' I replied.

Afghanistan is a poor country and the Hazaras are the poorest of the minority groups. They suffered politically, socially and economically in the late nineteenth century during the reign of Amir Abdur Rahman Khan, whose aim was to extend his power by force over the whole country. The Hazaras were the first ethnic group to revolt against him to maintain their independence from rule from the capital, Kabul. As a result thousands of Hazaras were killed and their women and children taken as slaves and concubines to wealthy Pashtuns. Having lost most of their fertile land, the

My early years in Afghanistan

Hazaras migrated to Kabul and other cities in Afghanistan, and to Iran and Pakistan where they made up the bulk of the unskilled workforce. In Kabul, the men worked as porters and labourers and the women worked as servants to the middle and upper classes. They were exploited and discriminated against, their work was hard and their wages low because they had become the underclass in Afghanistan. Those who have read the novel *The Kite Runner* by Khalid Husseini will have a clear picture of their position.

My own maternal grandmother, Mernisa, was a Hazara and my grandfather was from the Sayed line. In those days it was a privilege for a Hazara girl to be given as a gift to a man from a Sayed family, and so my grandmother was given in marriage to my grand-father although he was old enough to be her father. Hazaras have some of the features of Mongolian people – they have high cheekbones, round faces, light skin colour, and almond shaped eyes. My grand-mother was a devout Muslim, who never missed praying five times a day.

I used to visit my grandmother and stayed over-night, sharing her bedroom. She was a wonderful story teller and her favourite were ghost stories. I was addicted to them, and, much as it scared me to death, I always wanted to hear more. I remember her telling me a very scary story about Jews. She forbade us to go near the street where many Jews lived because she thought they kidnapped Muslim children and ate

My grandmother, Mernisa, (centre) with my Aunt Zainab on the left and my sister, Jahantab, and my nephew Sayed Taher Shah

them on their holy days. We never socialized with Jewish families. When my sister and I crossed the road where they lived, we held hands and ran as fast as we could for fear of being kidnapped. Looking back it makes me sad to see how our elders created such hatred and division, and how ignorant we were.

I remember how my grandmother used to make a *khatm* as a routine part of her life. *A khatm* is a way of praying for help in times of trouble and the prayers can be made in different ways. I remember my grandmother would read a chapter of the Quran every day so by the end of the month she had finished all 30 chapters. Then she blessed sweets and nuts and gave them to children. At the end of each *khatm* she always cried. Once I asked her why she always wept if the *khatm* was supposed to make her happy by solving her problems. She said she had committed a terrible sin and was crying to God for forgiveness. She told me that when she was young and foolish she killed her first-born child. She was fourteen years old when she married my grandfather and came to live in Kabul, and she did not see her family during the year after her marriage. During this time she gave birth to a baby boy. Then her brother came to visit her and she was overcome with the shame of having a physical relationship with her husband. In a state of panic she quickly hid the little baby, who was just a few days old, in a wooden box and covered it with blankets. By the time her brother was gone she opened the box to find the baby was dead.

My grandmother gave birth to twelve children and ten of them died as infants. Just my mother and her sister, my Aunt Zainab, survived. All her life right up to when she died aged eighty, my grandmother thought she had not been forgiven for her sin. She always claimed to hear foot-steps and see ghosts who brought messages from the past, especially from her dead children. For example, if in a silent room a fly made a buzzing noise she would assume it brought some news from one of her children or relatives, or that it could be one of her ancestral spirits. As a young girl, I was influenced by her and believed in ghosts and spirits during my teenage years.

My father, Sayed Ali Shah, was my mother's second husband. Her first husband had died from cholera when her son, my half-brother, was only four years old. According to Afghan tradition, a wife was part of her husband's property like a piece of furniture, and when he died, her in-laws were in charge of her fate. My mother was forced to marry one of her brothers-in-law, a man several years younger than herself. If she had refused she would have been forced to give up her son, and would not have been able to maintain herself, so she had no alternative but to marry my father. I believe she suffered quietly all her life. I remember her as a tall, graceful lady with a strong sense of responsibility and the ability to fight for what she believed in.

My early years in Afghanistan

In addition to her son from her first marriage, Sayed Shah, she had three children from her second marriage, a son, Sayed Taleb Shah, and two daughters, my sister Jahantab and myself. I was the youngest in the family and was greatly loved by my mother.

I have my mother to thank for insisting that I should have a good education. My father thought education was wasted on girls and would only make us argumentative. He believed girls did not need to be educated as they should just get married and bring up children. Our home became a battlefield and it was my mother who won. My father gave in and my sister, who was three years older than me, and I started school. We were over the moon with excitement and I proved to be an excellent student finishing infant and primary school in four years instead of six. After this my father never again tried to stop my education, and as education was free for all children, the fact that we were poor did not prevent me from attending school.

My mother died of cancer before she was forty and I was just seven years old. After this, my father, who was not really capable of bringing up a family, suffered greatly. My Aunt Zainab, who did not have any children, adopted my sister, while my brother and I stayed with my father. It made me very unhappy to part from my sister, but I learnt to conceal my feelings as my father had no patience when dealing with a young child.

Although I lived with my father, Aunt Zainab was

Many years later, reunited with Aunt Zainab after 22 years of separation

like a second mother to me. She was very strict and insisted on checking my hair every week for lice and inspecting my clothes to make sure they were clean and tidy. I remember once she found I was wearing socks with holes in them and she nearly went mad. She also had a strong belief in Islam and the Holy Quran and used to teach us with great passion and energy. My sister was good at it but I found it difficult because I was very young and I could not understand a word of it as it was in Arabic. Once I was stuck with a difficult page and I tore the whole page out thinking my aunt would not notice. Of course she did and she was so cross she hit me. 'How are you going to answer to God for your sin?' Every night after that, I trembled with fear and prayed to God for forgiveness. When it was time to study the Quran, we used to wash ourselves, gently take the Holy Book with both hands and kiss it, sit cross-legged on the floor, cover our heads with scarves and then with the book on our laps, we would start to read. 'Quran is beautiful music – read it with *qira'at* (rhythm)' Aunt Zainab would say. She emphasized the pronunciation but never explained the meaning.

Life was not easy for my Aunt Zainab. She was married to a senator, Sayed Ismail Shah Lolengy, a wealthy man with two other wives and a dozen children. When she became his third wife, Zainab gave up her job as a nurse because her husband thought that it would damage his reputation to have a working wife. Then, seven months after their marriage he and twenty of his friends were arrested for involvement in a conspiracy to overthrow King Zahir Shah. They were all sentenced to life imprisonment but after seventeen years were pardoned and released. I did not understand the background to his imprisonment or whether he was guilty or not. When he was in prison my aunt went back to work.

Prisoners were not allowed to see any of their family except young children at times of religious celebration. I was the youngest in the family and so had the privilege of going inside the prison to see him. He was kept in barbaric conditions. His cell was tiny and had no window. The light was kept on day and night.

He was only allowed out to use the toilet and then he had to knock loudly on the door for the guard to escort him. Two big iron bars were fastened to his legs which made it difficult for him to stand and impossible to bend his knees. I always felt sorry for him as he could not pray in the normal way as a Muslim should. But even though it was sad to see him like this, I still looked forward to the visits as he would give me money and sugared almonds sent in to him by my Aunt Zainab.

The prisoners were forbidden to receive any letters or books, but on one occasion my aunt sewed a letter inside my socks and I smuggled it in. I do not know what was written on it but it made him cry. He sent a small note back hidden in the plait of my hair and after that she stopped writing to him. I have always assumed that he asked her not to write again.

After my mother died my father became restless and we moved several times within the city of Kabul. Living with him meant I had to learn to stand on my own two feet. I had to cook, clean, wash and do the shopping and by the age of nine or ten could do most of the things needed to run a home – all this as well as doing my school work. I was doing very well at school and always came first in my class.

Finally, my father decided that we should move to a small village on the outskirts of Kabul where it would be cheaper and there would be fresh milk, eggs and vegetables. It also occurred to him that I might become too friendly with boys in the city, whereas in a small village the possibility of meeting boys was non-existent. By the time I was fifteen we had bought a small mud house in a village called Vazeer Abad. I loved living in the country, in the middle of wheat fields.

There was only one problem. It was a long way for me to go to school in the city and I had to walk across the fields for nearly an hour to get to the nearest bus stop and then take the bus for about half an hour. We were the only newcomers to the village, and I was the only girl from the village who went to school and also the only one who went out unveiled, without covering her head. At this time in the cities it was common for women to be unveiled and many women went out to work, but this was not the case in the countryside.

Whenever I passed the villagers I could see the hostility in their eyes; they looked at me as if I was from another planet. Perhaps they thought that an unveiled girl was a sign of danger for their daughters but, much as they disapproved, they never tried to harm me. We had bought our house from the officially appointed Malik, or village chief, and this afforded us a degree of protection. The Malik was usually the only one in the village who could read and write, and he used to sort out all the disputes between villagers.

The local men who were farmers and landowners led a very simple and relaxed life. They used to sit in front of their houses chatting and offering *naswar* to each other. *Naswar* is a weak powder of tobacco, which people put under their tongues for a few minutes before spitting it out. The young male villagers used to get up very early in the morning and go to the city to fetch manure from the open toilets. By nine or ten in the morning they were back, singing loudly as they walked behind their donkeys who carried the heavy fertiliser. This done they were free to laze in the sun and gamble with small dice made from dry mud. Gambling was officially forbidden in Afghanistan, but in the villages there was very little danger of being caught by the police.

The houses in the villages were built with a network of passages, yards and flat roofs, and some of them were shared with neighbours. From a distance the whole village looked like so many matchboxes, all stuck together. The authority of women inside the four walls of their house was unquestioned, but this did not apply outside the home. You would rarely see a young girl or woman walking in the village unchaperoned. They might be escorted by a brother, and even a younger brother could insist they did not go out and might give them orders as to how to behave. Most of the time women sat together on their flat roofs, sewing, gossiping and making *tappi,* flat cakes made from cow dung. They shaped them like plates and then put them in the sun to dry in the corner of the roof. The *tappi* were then used for winter fuel.

Life for these women was also simple; they were

kept separate and sheltered from outside influences. They were carefree and happily ignorant of what was going on outside the village. Outings were restricted to group visits to the *hammam* (public baths), or to weddings or to visit the shrine of a holy man. The women really enjoyed going to the *hammam,* where they all bathed together, naked apart from a small cloth wrapped around them, in a huge room full of water. They then moved to another room to rinse, and finally dressed in clean clothes for the trip back to the village.

Weddings were a great occasion where the women could show off their new clothes and jewellery. The women were separated from the men and preparations for the women's wedding party began seven or eight days beforehand, often continuing even after the wedding was over. Sometimes a wealthy host hired a band from Kharabad, the area in the old part of Kabul where self-taught musicians lived. The band would normally consist of four people: two women who sang and danced and two small boys who played instruments. Older boys were not engaged for the women's party. The two women who sang and danced painted their faces almost like circus clowns. The men's party was different. They dressed up a young man as a woman, put make-up on his face, and he danced all night long. Musicians played but none of the other men danced except this young man. This sort of party was banned by government law as it was considered immoral and thought to increase homosexuality, but in the villages nobody respected this law. It was easy to bribe the police and invite them to join in the festivities. Despite the fact that the villagers greatly enjoyed listening to the music, the musicians were still perceived as the lowest class, as it was believed that music was the voice of the devil and destroyed the Islamic faith.

The women loved visiting the shrine as a group. They wore their best clothes and make-up and even the younger girls were allowed to paint their faces like adults. In Afghanistan a shrine is the sacred grave of a holy man, usually one or two rooms decorated with colourful material, scarves and candles. Villagers believed that going to the shrine would solve their problems, so if a young boy wet his bed, a young girl suffered from depression or an old lady from arthritis, praying in the shrine would cure them.

No one was allowed to enter the shrine without removing shoes and visitors always put some money down for the caretaker, who sat outside reading from the Holy Quran and moving his head to and fro. The caretaker covered the walls and doors of the shrine with chain-like locks connected to one another. These rusty old locks had no keys and were closed. Whoever wanted a wish to come true moved the chain of locks repeatedly with their eyes closed, softly murmuring a prayer, and if during their prayer one of these locks opened, this was an occasion of much joy. It meant their prayers had been answered. The women hung beautiful scarves over the holy man's tomb and tied knots in the corner of the scarves to indicate they had a problem. If their wishes were answered they would untie the knots in the scarf and on the next visit there would be a gathering of friends and relatives. A big pot of *halwa*, a sweet food made from flour, oil, water, sugar and cardamom, would be cooked as a thanksgiving and portions given to the poor.

Seeing the sorcerer was another common practice among the village women, but not so common in the cities where people were more educated and less superstitious. The village women never admitted that they saw, or even knew the sorcerer, and always went individually, never as a group. This was because consulting a sorcerer was officially considered immoral, but desperate women always did so. If a possessive wife wanted to get rid of her husband's second wife, or an angry in-law wanted to damage the reputation of someone in the family, they would traditionally go to the sorcerer. He then supplied them with a *taweez*, a tiny bit of paper with Arabic words written on it in yellowish ink. They were told to keep the *taweez* in a hidden place for if it was found and opened, it would lose its effect. 'Keep it inside your husband's pillow,' he would say, or 'hang it in a tree to be moved by the wind,' or 'bury it in the ground or under the pavement'. The sorcerer always charged an amount of money small enough for the village women to be able to pay. I was fascinated by the difference in lifestyle between towns and villages.

Every morning on my way to school I passed a tiny, dilapidated old mosque which still attracted people to prayer. It had a deep well in the courtyard which supplied drinking water to the villagers. One day, without consulting my father, I decided that I would smarten up the mosque, so I bought some paint and enlisted the help of my two teenage nephews to paint the outside walls. I then made a framed sign for the mosque and my nephews hung it up outside. I did not do this for any reward or recognition, just because it was something positive I could do, and it really touched the hearts of the villagers. It had not occurred to them that an unveiled girl could be a good Muslim too. I heard that the Mullah, the religious leader, gave a speech about what I had done and also encouraged the local people to send their children to school. After that small gesture, the attitude of the villagers changed towards me and they became very friendly. One day, the Malik asked if I could teach his two daughters at home and I accepted without hesitation. From then on we had fresh milk and eggs from the Malik's house almost every morning. I felt at last my father was happy and perhaps would realize that having an educated daughter was not such a bad thing after all.

The following year I had many small children to accompany me through the fields to school and I felt like a heroine among my young friends. I lived in the village happily for the next six years and I will never forget the faces of those honest, trusting people.

Chapter Two
Marriage

I soar high into the atmosphere
A wonderful feeling
A wonderful dream
I fly far from the earth and I fly far from the hurt
Up and up I go and up some more
Light and happy as a feather

Throughout this time I continued my education and graduated from school to university. I finished school in ten rather than the usual twelve years and passed the school-leaving examination with good results. At that time, the government was encouraging both girls and boys to study, and school and university were free. At university we even got a payment to cover travel from home and books, as well as a sum of money when we completed the final dissertation. I studied a range of subjects, including history and geography, in my first year at Kabul University and in my second, third and fourth year specialized in journalism.

There were separate schools for girls and boys, but at university we were mixed together with roughly equal numbers of males and females in all classes. For all my subjects I was in mixed classes and I got used to talking to male as well as female students. One of my classmates was a very sociable student called Zafar who always had a lot of friends. During our first year of university I became aware that Zafar was attracted to me and was beginning to think of me as someone more than a classmate, and I also liked him – he was intelligent and great fun.

I was a dutiful Afghan girl, who had been brought up to consider her reputation, and I knew I had to stay away from him. My father always stressed this so it was planted in my mind from an early age. It never occurred to me to go behind my father's back so I did not allow myself any close friendship with the opposite sex. I even stopped talking to Zafar because I thought that if my father suspected I was having a relationship with a man, my university education would be stopped.

Eventually Zafar asked his mother to go to our house to ask my father to accept him as a bridegroom for me. I knew nothing about this plan. In our society it was thought respectful to approach a parent in this way. I knew my father well enough to know that he would refuse permission because of our Sayed root. Because Sayeds are descendants of the Prophet Mohammed, they do not allow their female children to marry outside the Sayed community because of preserving the purity of the blood. They believe that to introduce a male from outside brings disgrace on the family, but what I could never understand is that the restriction is not so strictly observed with the marriage of the male children. This did not make sense to me but it was not a subject I could have discussed with my father.

I was right and my father refused Zafar's mother and asked her not to call for this purpose again, but it is quite usual in our tradition to say no for the first, second and even third time of asking. If parents were to say 'yes' after only the first few visits it would be thought that they were letting their daughter down. People might think that they did not love her and wanted to get rid of her, or that she might have some fault or disability. The longer the process was prolonged, the more respect the daughter was thought to gain.

Zafar's mother continued her visits for a whole year. During all this time my father never asked me how I felt about Zafar. In an old-fashioned family like ours it was not easy for him to bring up the subject with his daughter. In the meantime, Zafar was becoming more and more frustrated as time dragged on, and he made up his mind to stage a silent protest against the fact that I would not speak to him and to highlight how determined he was to marry me. He stopped talking completely and would not speak a word to his family, relatives, friends, or even in our class at the university. When his teachers asked him a question he would write the answer on a piece of paper. His family thought he had been struck dumb at first, and tried everything to make him talk but eventually they realized the reason behind his silence. Our fellow classmates were very amused, but Zafar was not concerned. I was very embarrassed about the situation, but there was nothing I could do about it.

Zafar's mother continued to visit my father and on one visit she brought with her some elderly male relatives as a compliment to my father. My father told them that he could not give his daughter to a non-Sayed as it would bring shame on his family, and he would not be able to face his own people. These relatives then told him that Zafar was also a Sayed. My father, of course, asked them to produce a family tree and they agreed to do so.

About this time, when I came home from university I sensed an atmosphere in the house and decided to keep quiet. Later I found a copy of the *Kabul Times* in the kitchen. Although my father couldn't read or write, he liked to follow current affairs, so he would ask my brother to read out loud articles from the newspaper. I was surprised to see Zafar's picture at the bottom of the second page with a caption: 'Talkative university boy suddenly stops talking.' The article below detailed how he refused to speak because a certain girl would not talk to him out of regard for her family honour. Luckily it did not mention my name, but I felt my face go pale and my body turned to stone as I waited for my father's reaction, fearing that my university education was over. To my great relief, the next morning my father came into my room and told me gently that he was very proud of me for respecting the family honour and that I could continue at the university.

The next time Zafar's mother called she brought with her proof that Zafar's family were really Sayeds, and she was then offered tea and sweets. If someone visits an Afghan house, the host will usually serve tea and sweets unasked as it is not considered polite to ask guests first. But there was a special custom among old-fashioned families like mine – if the boy's parents went to the girl's house to seek her parents' permission to marry, the girl's family did not offer them tea or anything sweet until agreement was reached. So this marked the point when my father finally agreed that Zafar and I could marry.

In the autumn of 1966 we got engaged when I was nineteen years old and Zafar was twenty-six. He then broke his two months' silence and started talking normally again. In May of the following year we were married – it was a small wedding by Afghan standards but there were still over 100 guests. Then a new chapter of my life opened when I moved to the city to the large house where Zafar lived with his mother, his two married brothers, their wives and children, and his three unmarried brothers and sister. Living as part of an extended family was part of our tradition, and still is in many rural parts of

Marriage

Afghanistan. In an Afghan family, marriage does not mean the establishment of a new family but rather the extension of the two existing families. As a village girl I found it difficult to adapt to a large household full of people in the city, and no doubt they had some difficulty in adapting to me.

Zafar's great-grandfather was originally from Hamadan in Iran. Later in life he emigrated to India and settled in the Punjab. Before the partition of Pakistan and India, Zafar's father, Sayed Abdullah Shadji, rebelled against the British and fled to Afghanistan to avoid imprisonment. There he became very close to King Mohammed Nader Khan, the father of King Zahir Shah, and held high office in the government. Later, he started his own business exporting and importing goods from all over Europe. People used to say that if Shadji were to put his money in the Kabul River it would stop flowing. He was an influential man in his time, not just because of the power that came with his wealth but also for his concern for the poor. He helped many families to start their own businesses and to send their children abroad for higher education. He encouraged his children in their education, although unfortunately some did not live up to his expectations. He died before I married Zafar so I never knew him.

The extended family lived together in a huge bungalow, built behind a row of about nine shops which belonged to the family. I remember it had an enormously long, white marble corridor which was washed and polished every morning by the servants. All the ceilings in the house were decorated with fine, wooden carvings and almost every bedroom had an en-suite bathroom. The rooms were all carpeted with Afghan rugs. In addition to the rooms the family used, there was a large, beautifully furnished room for guests with a dining room adjoining it. The cupboards were packed with china and real silver cutlery. The massive garden was full of trees and flowers, and there were pears, grapes and blackberries growing there. The servants lived in a separate compound near our house.

Living with a number of in-laws is not always easy and can cause problems which may never be resolved. When I married Zafar I had two major faults in the eyes of his family. Firstly, I had come from a poor, working-class family – my father had a very small shop – into a rich, upper-class one, and some of Zafar's family felt that I did not merit this rise in class. Secondly, my grandmother was a Hazara and the mark of Hazara was clearly noticeable in me, from day one. Zafar's family thought I was inferior and did not allow themselves to think of me as a Sayed. One day I was shocked to see a black *taweez,* from a sorcerer, hanging in the big mulberry tree in our garden. I asked someone to take it down for me and found it covered by seven or eight layers of black cotton material. When I tore them off I discovered it was a wish for Zafar and me to divorce which we found very amusing and, of course, did not do.

At the beginning of my married life, I found the hardest part was dealing with the servants. In front of Zafar and his mother they were polite and obedient but it was very different when I was alone in the house with them. Once when my mother-in-law found me cleaning my bedroom she told me that was not my job. 'Why don't you get someone to clean it for you?' she said. I explained that I had asked but the servants said they were too busy. She called one of them and ordered her to clean and dust my room every day in future. Later, when I became friendly with one of the young servants, I learnt that they had been told not to do my work because I was a Hazara myself and Hazaras should serve, not be served.

However, Zafar's mother was always very good to me and I was very grateful to her for encouraging me to finish my university education. When our son, Yama, was born in 1968, my mother-in-law was a tremendous support looking after him while I studied. Although at that time we had plenty of helpers she would never leave Yama with them, but preferred to look after him herself so I knew he was in safe hands. After I finished my degree, I had a full-time job in the Ministry of Culture, compiling reference books. But the hours were long, so after a year I got a job as a teacher in the Institute for Women. The Institute for Women was established in the 1940s to provide an education for married women who had not completed school, as it was not considered proper for them to go to schools where they would mix with unmarried girls. This suited me well as classes finished at 1pm, so I had time to look after Yama in the afternoon. I taught Dari, history and geography, and enjoyed teaching women of about my own age.

Unfortunately, my mother-in-law died three years after I got married and it was as though I had lost my mother for the second time. After her death, I found it hard to live in a household with all the in-laws together. It took me some time to find my place as some of them had sharp tongues, and spread untrue stories about me which hurt my sensitive feelings.

One day I was sitting in the garden enjoying the sunshine and talking to the small daughter of one of our maids. Suddenly she asked me, 'Why did you give your ring to your father?'

I was stunned by her question. 'Which ring was that?' I asked.

'The big ring you had on your finger before you went to America,' she answered innocently with a smile on her honest little face.

In 1971, I was on holiday in Boston, USA, with Zafar and Yama who at that time was just three years old. One beautiful sunny day we went for a walk in the park. Suddenly a boy appeared in front of us, snatched my handbag and ran away through the woods. My engagement ring was in that bag and it contained a very valuable diamond that had been given to me by my mother-in-law. She had asked me to treasure it as it had a long history and I was terribly upset because, aside from the value of the ring, I felt I had failed my mother-in-law. She had given me the ring against the advice of some other members of the family and now I had lost it.

'I did not give that ring away. It was stolen in America,' I replied to the little girl. 'Why? Who told you I had given it to my father?' I asked her gently.

It was then she told me that she had overheard two of my in-laws talking amongst themselves and saying that I had given my engagement ring to my father to help him buy a new house. I was extremely hurt on hearing this but I never said a word. There seemed no point in trying to put the record straight, so I kept my feelings to myself.

At this time, Zafar was working as a freelance journalist for the independent *Caravan* newspaper in Kabul. Then he applied for a Fullbright scholarship to go to America for three years to study for a Master's degree. In 1972 my daughter, Parissa, was born and four months later Zafar left for San Francisco, while I stayed in Kabul. This was a difficult time for me living in Zafar's extended family without him, and it also meant the children hardly knew him. When he returned three years later, Parissa saw this huge man towering above her and refused to go near him. She could not believe this was her father.

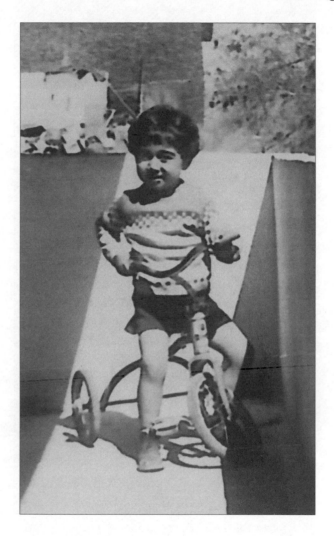

Yama on his tricycle in Kabul

Marriage

Parissa in Kabul

Yama, Parissa and I in Kabul

Living with in-laws can be a complete nightmare for the bride if there is an undercurrent of rivalry for the attention of her husband between her and her in-laws. This often happens if the husband is the eldest son in the family, who, after his father, is considered the head of the house and expected to be responsible for his parents in old age. However, I was fortunate that my mother-in-law always treated me well, and Zafar loved me very much. Living within an extended family has many advantages once you find your place. I was never worried about my children when I went out as everyone was responsible for caring for them. If they behaved badly family members had every right to tell them off, and I never asked why because I knew they loved them and had their best interests at heart. It was also great fun going out together as a large family group to the movies, parties or afternoon tea. In an extended family you never feel lonely as there is always somebody to talk to.

My first years of marriage were mainly happy ones, despite the death of my mother-in-law and Zafar's three-year absence. I had two children whom I loved, and I enjoyed my job as a teacher. But then my life and Zafar's were suddenly changed completely by the turbulent political situation which cast a shadow over family life.

Chapter Three
Communism and invasion

They invaded my rest
They destroyed my land
Who should I trust, where do I turn for help?
I am mortally wounded
Like a seagull that fell out of the sky
I perch on a twig
In the winter wind
I have no home
I am cold

I do not know exactly what went on behind the closed doors of those in power in the early days of the 1960s or even before that. But I know that it has led to the tragedy of a nation which is still continuing today, with many millions killed, made homeless or scattered throughout the world, innumerable disabled people, women without husbands and children without parents. What I have written is an honest eyewitness account of the human tragedy which befell my nation.

It would be unrealistic to put the blame for pushing Afghanistan into the mouth of the superpower Russia and the resulting civil war onto one particular group.

Communism and invasion

The causes are complex. There was certainly disharmony and hatred within the royal family which weakened the monarchy. The intense rivalry between the king, Zahir Shah, and his cousin and prime minister, Mohammed Davoud, gave their enemies every opportunity to attack the constitutional regime. The king, once a symbol of national unity and regarded by Afghans as 'the shadow of God', began to lose his power. The clerics, who had always been influential, misused their knowledge of Islam because the majority of them were poorly educated.

Although I had benefited from a good education in Kabul, there was a lack of basic education throughout the country. Most people could not read or write and maintained a traditional lifestyle. In the cities, the young, educated minority replaced the traditional lifestyle with the materialism of the West – cars, clothes, films, music and alcohol – all in the name of freedom and democracy. The value of our traditional lifestyle was discarded too rapidly.

The city of Kabul witnessed the incongruous sight of young girls in very short mini-skirts walking the same streets as veiled women in *chaderi*, a tent-like garment which covers the whole body and has a small window-like piece of embroidery in front of the eyes. In Shahr-i Naw, an area popular with upper class families, the increase in night clubs changed the atmosphere of the place and the behaviour of young people. These clubs, owned by the wealthy who had connections to high government officials, became centres of corruption and adultery. Ordinary citizens brought up in a conservative manner did not dare whisper any criticism and just shook their heads in disbelief. The clerics became very alarmed at this sudden introduction of a modern and un-Islamic lifestyle. Superficially, Kabul looked a bit like Paris or London because our merchants were filling the shops with Western products such as perfumes, lipsticks, clothes, shoes, fashion magazines and wild movie posters. Underneath everything was empty and dark; what we needed was better education, healthcare and living conditions for the majority of the people.

Zafar and I were both part of the educated minority, but Zafar allowed himself more freedom from traditional ways than I did. I remember we were invited to an evening party at the Intercontinental Hotel around 1966. The guests were a mixed bunch of senior Afghan officials and foreign diplomats. The alcohol was flowing like water and Afghan women were dancing in the arms of the men. In Western culture this is perfectly acceptable but to Afghans, used to traditional ways, it was unreal and unacceptable. For me, coming from a strict background, it was the first time I had experienced this kind of gathering. I was very embarrassed and refused to dance. In contrast, Zafar enjoyed every minute of the party and criticized me for not being more sociable. Our evening ended in a big row and we did not speak for a week.

Bribery and corruption became commonplace. A friend of mine was nominated for a six-year scholarship to America, and passed the required examination. She waited a long time to hear whether she had got the scholarship. In the end she went to the Exterior Ministry to find out what had happened, but she was told to wait and that the result would be sent to her in due course. She heard nothing and she later discovered that her scholarship had been sold to someone with the same name for about 12,000 Afghanis (a lot of money at that time).

In addition to these problems within Afghanistan there was also conflict with our neighbour, Pakistan. At the beginning of the 1960s, when Mohammed Davoud was prime minister, there was a lot of tension between Pakistan and Afghanistan over Pashtunistan. Pashtunistan is the area on the borders of Afghanistan and Pakistan which has long been disputed territory between the two countries. Pashtunistan used to belong to Afghanistan under Ahmed Shah Durrani in the eighteenth century. However, during the conflict with British India, King Abdur Rahman Khan signed a shameful agreement in 1893 giving up much of the territory to the British. The Durrand line was drawn between Afghanistan and British India, and Pashtun people were separated on either side of this line. This agreement was originally only for a hundred years but when the British left and the separate countries of India and Pakistan became independent in 1947, the issue remained unresolved.

Davoud was a nationalist Pashtun himself and during his time as Prime Minister he tried to get the land back. He stirred up tension by secretly giving aid to Pashtunistan nationalists and encouraging them to fight for their freedom from Pakistan. There was even an hour-long propaganda programme on Radio Kabul every evening, encouraging Pashtunistan to break away from Pakistan.

Because of this tension between the two countries, Davoud wanted to build a strong military base. He asked the USA for help but he was refused because America was allied with Pakistan. At that particular time, the cold war between America and the Soviet Union was at its height, so Davoud turned to Russia for help. The Soviet Union responded by granting military aid, arming and training Afghan military forces and educating many Afghan professionals and students in the Soviet Union. This was the start of growing Soviet influence and military support for Afghanistan.

At this stage King Zahir Shah did not have a good relationship with Davoud because the prime minister became more and more self-serving and arrogant. The king fired the prime minister in 1963. The Grand Assembly passed a law that no one could be prime minister from the royal family, and the king supported this law. Animosity between two cousins reached an all-time high. Ten years later, in 1973, King Zahir

Shah's reign came to an end when Davoud overthrew him, changed the constitution from a monarchy to a republic and made himself president without an election.

The first communist political party had been secretly created in Kabul under the name of the People's Democratic Party of Afghanistan (PDPA) in the early days of the 1960s. At that time, most ordinary people were either unaware or uninterested in the small gatherings of communists in the capital, Kabul. In 1965 the PDPA won a few seats in the parliamentary election and attracted more people in the other cities. In 1969 the party spilt into two branches, Khalq (mass) led by Noor Mohammed Taraki, who were mainly Pashto speakers, and Parcham (flag) led by Babrak Karmal, mainly Dari speakers. The two branches developed separately with growing hostility towards each other. In 1977 they reunited under the influence of the Soviet Union in preparation for the coup of April 1978.

In 1976 Zafar came back from America, and returned to work for the independent *Caravan* newspaper as a journalist. He became increasingly concerned about the unstable political situation and the sudden rise of the communist PDPA party – he was strongly anti-communist. I was not involved in politics at all, and my life was taken up with teaching and looking after our family, but I was very worried about Zafar who I feared would get into trouble for his anti-communist views as the PDPA became more and more powerful.

When Davoud first came to power he had a close relationship with the PDPA, and especially with Karmal's branch, although in fact Karmal was actively working under cover against the President. When Davoud realised that the Soviet Union was too involved with the PDPA, he travelled to Islamic countries for military aid but it was too late, as many Afghans who had trained in the Soviet Union were already in the army which was by now heavily Soviet dominated.

There was opposition to the Davoud regime from both branches of the PDPA, and matters came to a head with the murder of Mir Akbar Kyber, a high-ranking member of the party, in April 1978. The party accused the government and gained considerable publicity for its cause but there were also rumours that he had been murdered by one of his own party in order to bring about chaos. By this time Zafar and I and the children had moved to a block of flats in the Mecrorayon district of Kabul and Kyber's funeral procession passed just a few yards from where we were living. It was followed by a massive demonstration of thousands of party members through the streets of Kabul.

The next day the government ordered the arrest of some of the PDPA members, unaware that a coup was being planned. Then, on 27 April 1978, the PDPA took control of the Ministry of Defence and the national radio station, and started bombing the royal palace. We heard the first bomb explode in the palace where Davoud and his family lived and it sent shocks over the whole area. My daughter Parissa fell off the chair she was sitting on and hit her head on the floor. The bombing went on and on for hours and the smoke filled the skies of Kabul. We were all in shock. My children held their hands over their ears so as not to hear the terrible sound of the bombing, so I made them earplugs out of cotton wool.

President Davoud and his family and bodyguards were killed. The PDPA broadcast a short announcement that power was in the hands of the Revolutionary Council of the Armed Forces. Noor Mohammed Taraki became president and prime minister of the Democratic Republic of Afghanistan, with Babrak Karmal and Hafiezullah Amin as deputy prime ministers. They signed a treaty of friendship with the Soviet Union and Soviet aid increased.

In early 1979 the American ambassador, Adolph Dubs, was kidnapped in Kabul by men wearing police uniforms. They took the ambassador to Kabul Hotel and demanded the release of the Islamic prisoners. The staff of the embassy tried to convince the government not to fire, but they did, and the ambassador and the kidnappers were all killed. No one knew for sure who was responsible for the kidnapping. The government blamed Islamic supporters and vice versa. The result was that all American teachers and project workers left the country. This marked the end of American involvement in Afghanistan as Russian influence increased.

We were all stunned. It had happened so fast. Suddenly we realised that we were trapped in the grip of a superpower. Some blamed Mohammed Davoud for accepting Soviet aid, some blamed King Zahir Shah for being weak, others remained neutral and just watched the confused situation. A very strange atmosphere prevailed. Fear became stronger as the *Khad*, the secret police, became more and more powerful.

Following the execution of President Mohammed Davoud and his family, their entire possessions were shown at an exhibition for all to see. My curiosity led me to that exhibition and in it I saw the most tragic display of the dead children's clothes and toys. There was a beautiful Persian rug with a portrait of Davoud woven into it. It was being used as a door mat, an insult to the fallen president. I could not bring myself to wipe my shoes on this rug, and as I jumped over it I was aware of the soldier's glance, but he just smiled at me. It tore at my heart to see the disrespectful way the dead were being treated.

As soon as the communists seized power they began to apply their own ideology. Their first target was the religious leaders who were imprisoned and killed. Radio and television were controlled, the free press banned and opposition to the regime was forbidden. Zafar refused to tolerate these restrictions and this made it impossible for him to continue to work as an independent journalist, so he took a job as an English interpreter in the Libyan Embassy.

It seemed that every word we uttered was liable to be censored. Throughout the country, unconditional obedience was demanded. Each area had its own party headquarters and those who had been given authority to carry arms wore red armbands. Communist posters and slogans were on every street. Thousands of ordinary people were accused of being enemies of the regime and threatened with death. Spying on one another and regular meetings where people were denounced as enemies of the state became a normal part of life. We did not dare to trust or talk to each other. Parents were afraid of their children and could not talk about the regime in front of them because many young people were indoctrinated in the communist youth clubs and might report their relatives.

In every school, children were divided into two groups – the left and the right. The left group had more favourable treatment and were expected to report on what was going on in homes and neighbourhoods, and how parents and neighbours felt about the revolution. The headteacher had the special task of keeping watch on the students. Some teachers and headteachers who had been under suspicion were replaced by young and inexperienced teachers who were trusted by the communists. Religious teachers were automatically labelled anti-government and people became confused about right and wrong for they were now told that religion meant superstition. The word 'brother' which was the symbol of unity among Muslims was replaced by the term 'comrade', because comrades were more valued than brothers. This chaos was poisoning the hearts and minds of our young generation.

Parissa was too young to understand what was going on, but Yama was ten years old and was subjected to this brainwashing in school. Although he was not in one of the youth clubs at his school, his cousin (who lived in the same house as us) was. Both Zafar and I were very wary about discussing anything to do with politics in front of Yama in case he might pass on what we said to his cousin. We were not even safe in our own homes.

As a teacher, I hated myself for upholding the regime against my own beliefs but I had no choice. Every morning before lessons began we were obliged to line up all our students in front of the headteacher's room and sing the new national anthem loud and clear. The headteacher then gave a lecture about our president, Taraki, and his glorious regime. It bored us to death and we did not dare look at each other for fear of laughing, which would have meant getting our names on the black list. Then the teachers had to give another pep talk about our leader before starting to teach. The students had to answer questions such as: 'Where was the leader born? Who were his parents? What has he done? When did he join the party?' We also had to teach communist literature. In the staff room where previously we had enjoyed our fifteen-minute breaks we were careful not to say anything about the regime. If someone started to say something that could endanger her, we whispered the old Afghan proverb – 'the walls have mice and the mice have ears.'

Every few months, schoolteachers, children, office workers, manual workers and bank staff were forced to join a grand march through the main street of Kabul to denounce the 'bloodsucking imperialists and capitalists'. Most people had no idea what these words meant, but just knew they had to shout loudly and excitedly. Death was threatened to all capitalists but where were these capitalists? We had no idea. Teachers, students and even primary school pupils had to wave thousands of red banners and shout hurrahs to the leader. They called him 'the genius of the east'. The more they shouted, the more loyal they appeared and the more benefits would come their way.

There was a young boy whose father rented one of our shops for a minicab service. On one of the days the marches were taking place, he went with his school group to join the demonstration. Every one was shouting, 'Long live Lenin', the Russian leader.

The boy had no idea who Lenin was. He was shouting 'Long live nylon' instead, which sounded similar when pronounced by a Dari speaker. He was arrested by the *Khad* for making fun of the great leader and misusing his name purposely. His father was so worried that he asked Zafar for help. Luckily, Zafar managed to get him set free and we all laughed about it in the end.

Everywhere in all public buildings, restaurants, parks, cinemas, schools and offices you would see the slogan in red *'Coor-,calli- dodai'*, which means, 'House, clothes, bread', and under it the portrait of our leader. People were sick and tired of the red and sometimes, under cover of darkness, they would replace the leader's slogan with their own 'honour and freedom or death'. It was at this time that the red flag, the symbol of communism, replaced the traditional national flag which was red, black and green. It was declared a 'flag' day and thousands of people were forced into joining the celebrations. I could not believe my eyes as the sky was red with balloons, the walls were red with slogans and portraits, and the streets were full of bemused people holding red flags and portraits of our leader. Helicopters were dropping red slogans from above, all the cars and trucks were decorated in red and everybody wore red armbands. We walked from our school some five miles or so to where Taraki was standing with his cabinet by the gates of the royal palace, which was now called the 'people's house'. The headteacher told us that when we got near the leader and his cabinet we were to turn our heads towards him and vigorously wave our flags. Red was definitely the colour of the day.

We had a young neighbour called Naheed, whose husband became obsessed with the colour 'red'. He had been recruited into the party and, after a short time, his abilities were noticed and he was allowed to carry a gun. After the flag celebrations he bought a red curtain for their bedroom, then red clothes for the family, and so it went on. Eventually his wife had had enough and refused to wear any more red clothes, so he beat her regularly. One day he bought a tin of paint and covered everything in the kitchen, even the door and window, with red paint. Their once peaceful life had become hell. One morning after a fierce argument he left home for his office where he had another argument with his colleagues over the same issue, eventually lost his temper and killed four of his colleagues and then himself. His wife was left alone with four young children to feed. The memory of those innocent faces has stayed with me through all these years. Naheed was just twenty four when I knew her, like a butterfly caught in a thunderstorm.

Suddenly the small village of Nawa-e-Ghazni, which previously had been virtually unknown, became famous as the place where Taraki had been born. Poems and songs were written about this special place which had given us such a leader. One amusing thing was that the young who were enthusi-astic about the party trimmed their moustaches in exactly the same style as the leader's, while those who disliked Taraki shaved off the moustaches they had had all their lives.

Another amusing incident was the establishment of a museum quickly created to show the leader's childhood. His tiny clothes, his cradle, his parents' clothes and all their belongings were there. However, Taraki was born into a poor nomadic family and we asked each other how a nomad child and his parents, who were always travelling and always poor, had managed to keep their belongings intact for over sixty years. Perhaps he knew from the beginning of his childhood that he would be a great man!

People who had completed their higher education in Western countries were now automatically on a blacklist and if the government could manage to replace them they did not hesitate to do so. This made me very worried about Zafar. Those who had not finished their education were promoted to important positions if it suited the government. I had a very shy girl in my class, who was not one of my brighter students and was hardly able to answer a single question I asked her. She dropped out of college and when I heard that her husband had become the president's devoted bodyguard I assumed she must be very busy at home. One day during a school break I was sitting in the school garden when suddenly a small crowd of women attracted my attention. They were gathering around a black Mercedes. The driver opened the car door and a tall, well-dressed lady stepped out. 'Who might she be?' I wondered. When she reached the gate of the school I realized she was my student. It was not a great surprise as she had a famous husband, but I was shocked and disgusted to find she had just returned from a visit to Eastern European countries where she had been invited to conferences as the representative of the women of Afghanistan. I truly felt sorry at the complete corruption our country was facing.

Our libraries and museums were rapidly looted by their staff who probably knew their jobs would not last long. There was an ex-colleague of Zafar's called Rahimi who had worked with him on the *Caravan* newspaper. He had no family of his own and no regular job, making money as and when he could. During the Davoud regime he had been in prison for smuggling drugs out of the country. Now we heard he had a job with the *Khad,* the secret police, which was no surprise to us as he had very few principles. Once in the *Khad,* his financial circumstances changed rapidly, he moved into a luxury flat and drove a black Mercedes. One day he brought me some valuable books which were masterpieces of calligraphy. He asked me to cover them in some red velvet.

'Where did you get all these valuable books?' I asked him.

'I inherited them from my grandfather who died recently,' he answered.

I asked him why he wanted them covered and he replied, 'Because I need money. I want to sell them abroad and for extra protection they need to be covered.'

Later we discovered the books had been stolen from a museum and that Rahimi's grandfather had died when he was only six. He laughed sheepishly when I mentioned this to him and said, '*Hamsherra jan* (my dear sister), if my bosses can steal so can I.' I was stunned by his shameless answer and made no comment.

One day, while Zafar and I were watching television, we recognized a familiar face. The man was named Ashraf and he was talking animatedly on behalf of his ministerial office, denouncing and cursing the royal family and the previous regime, and calling them thieves. In the light of our own previous experiences with Ashraf, Zafar and I looked at each other and laughed. We knew Ashraf was a real crook.

Some years previously, in 1971, we had a few days in Moscow on our way to America for a holiday. Zafar wanted to change our money into roubles on the black market to get a better exchange rate than from a bank, and he met an Afghan student called Ashraf and his friend from Tajikistan who offered to help us. We all had dinner together and then the next day Zafar went off to change the currency and have dinner with our friends while I stayed behind at the hotel with Yama.

I heard nothing till one o'clock in the morning, when the sound of the telephone made me jump out of bed. It was Zafar on the line. He sounded very worried and said he did not know where he was. He then asked me to call the hotel manager to the phone, which I did. The manager was as puzzled as I was but he managed to figure out where Zafar was and called a taxi for me and gave an address to the driver. It was a very long drive in a strange country. I had a young child on my lap and I did not speak a word of Russian, but the taxi driver was a kind man and somehow I felt safe with him. Finally, he found the address and honked his horn, and Zafar came out accompanied by two Russian ladies.

Later Zafar told me the full story. After the two men had changed his money into roubles, Zafar realized they were drunk and they began quarrelling in Russian. All he could make out was the word for fifty per cent. Then they all had dinner with the two Russian ladies and after dinner Ashraf asked Zafar to go for a walk with him. One of the ladies pleaded with Zafar not to go and Ashraf lost his temper and pushed the woman. A big knife fell out of Ashraf's pocket and the other woman quickly threw it out of the window. Then Zafar realized that Ashraf was planning to kill him and to take his money. Asraf denied this, 'I am an Afghan and you do not trust me – you trust these filthy

Russians more than your own countryman.' He then stormed out with his friend following him. The next day when Zafar went to the university he found that no one there knew of anyone called Ashraf. He had had a lucky escape.

Years later, the editor of the *Caravan* newspaper where Zafar was working asked him to interview a young student named Mohammed Aman who had recently returned from Moscow. When Zafar saw it was Ashraf he refused to interview him, saying it was for personal reasons. Apparently his real name was Mohammed Aman not Ashraf. We found it very amusing to see him denouncing our previous government as thieves.

Because our leader, Taraki, the founder of the communist party in Afghanistan, was born into a nomadic family it was doubtful if he knew his date of birth, but in spite of this his followers celebrated his birthday with great publicity. This was strange as birthday celebrations are not a traditional custom among our people, although some members of the upper class and the monarchy, under foreign influence, had begun to celebrate birthdays. When a child was born into an Afghan family there was usually a party six days after the birth to which friends and family were invited. A mullah from the mosque or an elderly relative would read a few lines from the Quran to the child, than he would name the child and write the date on a piece of paper which was put inside the Holy Book. It did not seem to matter if this piece of paper got lost later. In fact some families did not record the date of birth at all. Once I asked my father how old he was and he did not know exactly, but he thought it was during the revolt against King Amanullah Khan. I was grateful to my Aunt Zainab for writing my date of birth in the corner of the Holy Book, for neither of my parents could read or write. More recently people in the cities have begun to think it is important for their children to know their date of birth, but celebration of the date was uncommon.

The preparations for Taraki's birthday lasted for weeks. The garden of the royal palace was illuminated by coloured lights and the inevitable red slogans decorated the walls. Representatives from all over the city were asked to join in the celebrations and all headteachers, and one or two students from the top class in each school and college, were also invited. Rahema, a pretty young woman with two children from my class at the Institute of Women, was delighted to be chosen to attend. But there was one problem. Her husband had not been invited. A month or two after the event I realized that Rahema had lost her sparkle and was looking very tired and unhappy. She stopped coming to college and I asked her best friend what had happened. I was told that Rahema's husband was divorcing her and taking the children to Pakistan because of what he had heard had happened at the palace on the night of the birthday celebrations. Once again this was a clash between tradition and the new values, to which the people had not had time to adjust. I felt very sorry for the young, pretty mother and wondered what would become of her.

At that particularly chaotic and unhappy time, there was anarchy and hatred among the people but our leaders were too drunk with power to see it. The oppressive atmosphere was becoming intolerable and slowly opposition began to grow both in Kabul and in the countryside. Many people, including doctors, engineers, artists, writers and journalists, tried to escape from the unbearable political situation. Some succeeded in getting out of the country, but others who were less fortunate were captured and imprisoned. Most families had relatives who were either missing or had disappeared over the border. Even in our own homes it was safer to talk only through facial expressions. People stopped going to the mosque for fear of being accused of anti-government activity.

My father had a cousin called Sayed Mansour Shah who was a devout Muslim. He knew nothing about politics and was well known for his honesty. One evening two uniformed men knocked at his door and asked him to go with them to answer some questions. He went with them as he was, without shoes or jacket. He never came back. His sons looked for him everywhere, in every prison, but there was no trace. He seemed to have vanished from the face of the earth. His wife was heartbroken and died from a heart attack soon after and his sons are scattered across the world as refugees.

The short-lived coalition between the two factions of the party broke up. Taraki and the deputy prime Minister, Amin, scattered members of the Parcham faction by sending them out of the country and Babrak Karmal was sent to Prague as ambassador. While Taraki was away in Havana on a visit, Amin had full authority to kill and imprison as many innocent people as he could. He appeared on television almost nightly and created terror in the hearts and minds of the people. When Taraki returned from Havana via Moscow, his arrival was another day of orchestrated flag-waving and riotous cheering, but within a few days of his return the close partnership between Taraki and Amin turned to enmity. In September 1979 Amin seized power and suffocated Taraki, whom he had previous called his 'great teacher', with a pillow. The faithful student had turned out to be the most unfaithful. It was announced on television that Taraki had died from a rare and undiagnosed illness. The news about his death was shorter than a brief advertisement. There was no talk about his past or even of a funeral service for the man who had been such an acclaimed leader, although the magnificence of his home-coming from Moscow and his flamboyant birthday celebration were still fresh in the minds of people.

Under Amin things were even worse. Although the slogans, 'House, clothes, bread' were replaced with 'Law, security, justice', this was never implemented. The Pull-e-Churki and Demazang prisons held 75,000 prisoners under inhumane conditions. We were all in terror of the *Khad*. When my friend Sarah's uncle was murdered in prison, the family was not allowed to hold a funeral for him. The body was released on condition that it was buried under cover of darkness in complete silence. Usually after a funeral, the memorial service lasts three days, but this did not happen in this case. A few days later when I went to see Sarah I was extremely upset and started to cry loudly, but she put her hand over my mouth to stop me from making the slightest sound. She was terrified of what the *Khad* would do if she broke the condition for releasing her uncle's body.

The news of Taraki's death and his replacement by Amin shocked the Soviet Union. The Soviets were opposed to Amin who had not shown himself to be a loyal supporter, and so they decided to intervene openly in Afghanistan to overthrow him. Within a few days, on 27 December, a group of Soviet commandos attacked Darulaman Palace where Amin lived, and killed Amin and his family. The voice of Babrak Karmal was heard on radio Dushanba, broadcasting from Russia, declaring himself to be the new leader of Afghanistan. He accused Amin of having been an agent of the American Central Intelligence Agency

(CIA). But it was too late for Babrak to be accepted by the Afghan people. He was too closely associated with the communists and the discredited previous regime to offer any real hope of change. The people of Afghanistan had already made up their minds not to trust him, recalling the old proverb, 'The yellow dog is the jackal's brother.' Zafar and I waited nervously by the radio to hear Babrak speak. Zafar was pacing up and down the room holding the radio, full of anger with the communists for taking away our freedom.

Babrak arrived in Kabul accompanied by Soviet soldiers. He took power in a matter of days and exposed how Amin and his followers had been responsible for the suffocation of Taraki. We heard them admitting their shameful act on the radio. He released thousands who had been held in the notorious Pull-e-Churki prison. The opening of the gates was shown on television, and we saw crowds of people rushing in and out, desperately hoping to find their loved ones. This was another extraordinary day for Afghanistan. The self-appointed government posted on the wall of the Interior Ministry a long list of about 15,000 names of people who had been executed at the order of the previous leaders. I went with my friend Simeen whose father and brothers had disappeared, to give her moral support. She found her father's name on the list but her two brothers had vanished. To this day no one knows what happened to them. We saw a young man who had found his father's name on the list – he was crying and banging his head on the wall. He claimed that his father had still been alive after Babrak came to power and was shouting that the new leader was a killer. He was surrounded by people trying to calm him down.

By this time there was a lot of opposition to the communist regime and to the Russian soldiers who were now based in Afghanistan. There was a day of mourning fixed for the people of Kabul to mourn those killed under Taraki's and Amin's leadership, and women members of the communist party were sent to the homes of mourners to share their sorrow. One of my students – a young woman called Hameda – arrived at school next day with a scar on her face. Apparently her next-door neighbour was a woman with a dozen children whose father had been killed by the communists. They were having a desperate struggle to make ends meet and, when the party members called at her door, the woman shouted: 'You whores of Russia killed my husband and now you come with sympathy. I do not need your sympathy. I need food for my children.' Hameda heard them and found the woman brawling with the visitors. She placed herself between them and was slightly injured. She told me the two women ran away as fast as they could and did not look back. Hameda found it all very amusing, but to me it was another sad story of our time.

One day there was a rumour in Kabul that people were going to stand up and show their opposition to communism and atheism. We could not believe such a thing was possible. How did people muster up the courage to do this and what exactly was going to happen? It was ten o'clock when the regular curfew started and people had to be at home. The city died and all the lights were turned off. At first a few voices were heard coming from the roof tops shouting, 'Allah-o Akbar' (God is great). We do not want this Godless regime. We do not want Shah Shoja again.' Shah Shoja was the King of Afghanistan from 1830 to1840. He was backed by the British and agreed to accept British control over his foreign policy and to grant them territory in return for money. This was the worst treaty made in our history. In consequence, the British had to face a disastrous loss and suffered terrible hardship, and Shah Shoja lost his life. The voices became louder and stronger, ringing out from almost every roof top in town. Zafar and I fearfully climbed onto our roof top to join in and shouted for a long time until the noise finally died down. That night we went to bed with fear in our minds about what would happen the next day. A group of protesters were imprisoned but it was impossible to arrest all those who had joined in.

The new government tried to heal the pain of the people, but the feeling against the communists was now so strong that all their efforts failed. Resistance groups started all over the country challenging the government. A bloody war began as hatred grew stronger and spread more widely. The Russian troops were particularly hated. On my way to the college I used to see an old man near the Haji Yaqqub mosque selling dried mulberries and walnuts. One day when I was passing I saw a Russian soldier shouting at him angrily but when I came close the Russian walked away, so I asked the old man what had happened.

'I am not selling my mulberries to a white pig even if I die of starvation,' he said.

'Good for you,' I thought. Like many people I knew that a superpower was not going to take over our hearts and minds, even if they had superiority in arms. No one liked the Russians except the puppet government which was under the thumb of the Soviets. Afghan people never mixed with the Russians despite the fact that it is part of our culture to be hospitable and friendly. We never talked to them, never asked them to have a cup of tea with us or shared our food.

In Kabul the Russian officers and advisers resided in the best area called Mecrorayon, where we lived. I used to see them walking around in the late afternoon with sullen faces. The only people who would talk to them were salesmen selling vegetables from their donkeys. Everything the Russians bought they had to bargain for and they always looked for the cheapest. It must have been hard to live in a foreign country where they were so hated, but their government left them no choice.

Communism and invasion

I read later how Russian soldiers were sent to Afghanistan against their will and how devastated their families were when they heard they had lost loved ones in the war. One soldier was told he had been selected because of his technical skills to join a group working to maintain tank engines, but first the group would be sent by plane to another part of Russia to help with the harvest. When the soldiers discovered this was a lie and they were being sent to fight in Afghanistan, they were overcome with fear, and, drunk with vodka, tried unsuccessfully to escape. They were thrown back into the plane which took off for Afghanistan, where they had no option but to fight in the Soviet army. Their families were told they had volunteered.

At the beginning of the invasion, Russian soldiers were not involved directly in the war against the resistance, but the government soon became desperately short of fighters so Soviet troops, as well as university students and school boys from the higher classes, were enlisted. Many people wanted to leave the country to avoid being recruited into the army. Some succeeded but others failed and soon all shops, streets, markets, parks, cinemas and restaurants were empty of young men.

Zafar's family owned a number of shops in front of our house and in one of them there worked a young assistant called Sattar, who came from Pajsheer, a city in the north of Afghanistan. He was not able to visit his family very often and I always felt sorry for this young, hardworking boy. He looked so sensitive and was always polite. The shopkeeper and his young assistant used to lay their tools out on the pavement near the shop and repair punctured tyres. The poor boy was in an agony of anxiety every day seeing soldiers in the distance heading towards the shop. He used to creep into our house and we would keep him indoors until all was clear again. My young children became great friends with Sattar. Finally he was caught by a soldier. He pleaded that he was too young, but the soldier pulled down his trousers and looked carefully at his legs. After what seemed like an eternity, the soldier decided he was old enough to be recruited because his legs were hairy. My heart was bleeding, but there was nothing I could do.

Two weeks later we got a call from Sattar to say he was leaving Kabul for the south of the country with a group of soldiers. My children were very upset. Then my sister-in-law thought of a daring plan to help the boy. The next morning she and I took a taxi to see Sattar. When we got to the camp, our taxi stopped in a side road quite near the iron gate of the camp. I stayed in the taxi and my sister-in-law went up to the guard who was sitting inside a booth near the gate and asked if she could see her son Sattar before he left. After a long wait, Sattar came out and sat down with my sister-in-law in full view of the guard. Then they got up and moved a bit further away and sat down again. Again after a little while they moved slowly further away. Suddenly they ran as fast as they could. Before the guard could reach them they were in the taxi and we raced off. That afternoon Sattar left Kabul for good and two years later I saw him in Pakistan. He was happy to be fighting under the command of one of the leaders of the resistance, Ahmed Shah Masoud. Masoud fought against the communists and later the fundamentalist Islamic Taliban regime and was finally killed by the Taliban, two days before the bombings in America on 11 September 2001,

When Dr Najibullah, the imperious chief of the *Khad*, replaced Babrak Karmal in 1986 we were fortunately out of Afghanistan, but we heard that the government was facing dissent. Najibullah denied being a communist and tried hard to change government policy, particularly with regard to religion. He went to mosques and prayed with the people, telling them that they should not be afraid. He pretended he was a believer, but the strange thing was there were no mullahs left in the country. The government was desperate to replace them. We once had a doorman called Amrollah who we used to call Baba (father) Mullah. He had been with us since my father-in-law was in his prime and stayed with us all his life, remaining loyal towards all the family until we left and there was no one for him to serve. Later I heard from my sister-in-law that the government had taken

Amrollah to the mosque to preach to the people. He had a long white beard and was always dressed in white. The poor man must have been in a very awkward position for, although he was a decent man and said his daily prayers, he had no great knowledge of Islam.

Afghan politics is a complex subject and, although I always sympathized with Zafar's opposition to the communist regime, I never shared his strong opinions. Politics is not really 'my cup of tea', as the British put it, and during these turbulent years my main concerns were looking after my family and my work as a teacher. But now I see what a disaster the communist regime was for Afghanistan.

Many Afghans call the supporters of the communist regime *watan-froosh*, meaning 'selling the country to foreigners', which in our language is one of the worst possible insults. Despite all the tragedies that happened to our family and friends, I would not use the insult *watan-froosh*. Looking back, I believe the communists were led by a group of energetic young men, adventurers, university educated, who were influenced very much by the Russian Revolution. They wanted to bring about quick reforms to the corrupt system of the government and were unaware that the deeply religious and traditional culture of most Afghans would make rapid change difficult. Their model was based on our northern neighbour, Russia, who had been waiting for this opportunity to gain power in Afghanistan for so long, in order to gain a strategic position against the Americans.

They did not have enough experience in running the government. They used their frenzied, frightening power against Islam and to introduce land reform, neither of which had the support of the nation. And most of all, the rivalries and enmities among their own party played a big part in the collapse of the regime and the invasion of Afghanistan by the Soviet Union. We were, and still are, far away from the socialist regime they claimed to be. They called it revolution but it was really a military coup that resulted in the catastrophe of long-term civil war, the creation of the Taliban and the violence we see today. Zafar and I and the children, like many others, were unfortunate enough to be caught up in these terrible political events.

Chapter Four
Zafar in prison

Oh my dear God
Open a tiny window of your light
I am weeping in silence tonight
From the throat of a woman
From my ruined land
Whose body crumbled
Under the pebbles and sand
What does justice mean
Under the weight of cruelty
Not knowing where to flee
Oh my dear God
Let me be free tonight
From the thought of those who lost justice
In a deep ocean of blood, anger and starvation
Oh my dear God
I am weeping tonight

After the communists came to power and took control of the media, Zafar found a job as an interpreter in the Libyan Embassy as it was impossible for him to continue working as an independent journalist. But he continued to write critical articles against the communist regime and circulate them among people he knew, although this was very dangerous and if the *Khad* had got hold of any of these articles we would all have been killed. Zafar was passionate about what he believed in and undeterred by the dangers of criticizing the regime.

One day when he was at work, he was suddenly summoned to the office of the Minister of Information and Culture, Bariq-Shafie. Zafar knew Bariq from his time as a parliamentary correspondent for the prestigious and independent *Caravan* newspaper, but he had no idea why he had been sent for on this occasion. We were both very worried that someone had reported him for writing against the regime. It was therefore with some trepidation that Zafar went to see Bariq, but to his surprise he was offered a top job in the communist government. He was given a week to consider the offer but he knew from the outset that he would refuse. When the week was up he wrote a short letter explaining his position carefully and politely declining the post. Two months later, Zafar was suddenly sacked from his position at the Libyan Embassy. The Libyan Ambassador said he was very sorry but he could not jeopardize his own relationship with the government by continuing to employ Zafar.

It was dangerous for Zafar to stay in Kabul, so in 1979 he found a temporary job as a clerk in a small building project in Towraghondi in Herat, a province in north-west Afghanistan, while I stayed in Kabul with the children. One evening a small group of workers were having a friendly chat which eventually led to a political discussion. It did not occur to Zafar that there could be any danger in this small village far from Kabul and he spoke out freely against the communists. The next morning he was approached by one of the other workers who had taped the discussion and now wanted money to keep quiet about it. Zafar refused to submit to blackmail and eventually the boss of the company, who was a puppet of the communists, came to hear about what Zafar had said. Zafar was tied to his bed and beaten and then left without food for ten days. He paid the price for his careless talk by losing four front teeth. He was also sacked. He took it philosophically but I did not.

Zafar came back to Kabul and continued to write against the regime. Every night I begged him to stop writing but he was determined to continue. In the end I couldn't take it any more. I went to his study late one evening while he was typing and demanded a divorce if he did not stop putting his family in danger. I was well aware that a Muslim woman should not mention divorce to her husband unless she really meant it, and I did mean it. I had never been more serious. Although I was sympathetic to his philosophy, he was endangering the lives of our children and they were my first concern.

Soon afterwards Zafar gave up writing. One night he sorted his papers into two piles. One pile he burned, the other he buried at the end of our garden. It was just in time. Two weeks later we were visiting my sister when we had a telephone call from my sister-in-law, warning us not to come home. Our house had been raided by the *Khad* and the under-cover police were everywhere. My stubborn husband of course went home, but the children and I stayed with my sister for the night. We returned the next morning convinced that Zafar had been taken into custody, but surprisingly I found him still at home. The *Khad* had turned the whole place upside down, but luckily had not found anything incriminating. However, they took all our books, cassettes and even our photographs – I am not sure why. I started to clean up the mess, full of relief that I had taken a stand two weeks ago and that Zafar had got rid of all his writings.

It was a very difficult time and I could see that Zafar was beginning to suffer from stress. Something was wrong with him. He became more and more impatient. He was restless, unable to sleep and his behaviour became very odd. Then at the end of August 1980 a friend called me to say that Zafar had been taken to the *Khad* office. I had feared this would happen sooner or later.

Zafar was in prison for three nights and was then released. At this time I had no idea why he had been imprisoned, as he was incapable of rational conver-sation. When he came home he was even more agitated, sleepless and hyperactive, and was losing touch with reality. He developed a mania for holy things. Every day he thought he was someone different, rather than his real self. One day he was a prophet, the next a genius, and on one occasion he was God.

He began to talk non-stop about religion, politics and the Russians. He claimed to have visions and conversed openly with non-existent people. One stormy night he woke me from a deep sleep to tell me that I should not be worried as he could control the wind. He then started to read loudly from the Quran. He tried desperately to make me understand what he was raving about. By this time I realized he was having a serious mental breakdown.

His brother and I contacted the hospital and two men came to take him away. They had to restrain Zafar who tried to resist. He was admitted to a mental hospital, where he was first put in a large ward full of very disturbed people, all of whom were locked in. Visitors were not allowed in to visit the patients while they were so disturbed and violent, and could only see them through a large barred window – screaming and fighting amongst each other. A huge, long-haired man sat on the window sill and if the patients made too much noise he was allowed to beat them. They were given no medicine until they had calmed down in their own time. Then the doctor separated them and gave them tranquilizers.

Zafar in prison

I visited Zafar every day hoping that his condition would improve, but it remained the same for a long time. I was not allowed near him when he was violent. I just had to watch him from a distance through iron bars. One day when I was visiting him I saw him tear off his shirt and use it as a prayer mat, reciting verses loudly from the Quran. Amazingly the other men in the ward all followed his example. This performance was heartbreaking to witness as this was not the Zafar I had married. I remembered him in his prime at university, full of joy and mischief, the cleverest in the class with a bright future ahead. He had a characteristic way of speaking and joking that made him stand out among both his friends and teachers. He was always expressing his opinion on some interesting subject, surrounded by other students. Now seeing him as a mental patient, I could not keep back my tears.

One day Zafar's brother went to see him. He did not want to believe that Zafar was really mentally ill, and when he came back from the hospital he told me not to worry because his brother was just acting as if he was mad to fool the authorities. I did not contradict him but his quick diagnosis hurt me very much. I knew my husband better than anyone and was certain he was very sick indeed. A week later my brother-in-law and his family escaped to Pakistan and then on to Germany. I felt that he was making out that Zafar was faking illness in order to put his own conscience at rest for leaving us behind. Under Afghan custom, his brother should have supported me and the children, if Zafar was too sick to do so himself.

Zafar was in hospital for about two months and this was a dreadful time. Even as I write about those events of long ago, the pain is still in my heart. Eventually Zafar calmed down as a result of all the drugs he was given and was discharged from hospital. With the change in environment he gradually improved and finally regained his sanity. He was able to recall perfectly the events which led him to be taken to the *Khad* office in the first place. Some Russian soldiers had thrown their empty beer cans into the road and Zafar, who was always impulsive and often acted without thinking, foolishly told them to pick up their rubbish. He reminded them that they were in Kabul, not in Russia, and they took offence. There was an argument and within minutes Zafar was surrounded by a group of soldiers who marched him off to the *Khad* office. He was kept there for three days with nowhere to sleep, and on the third night a Russian officer appeared with an interpreter and began to question him.

Zafar told him, 'I did not commit any crime and I don't feel obliged to answer a foreigner in my own country. I want to talk to an Afghan officer.' Fortunately the Afghan interpreter did not translate this accurately and changed it to a version that was acceptable to the Russian. It was obvious that the Russian officer was still suspicious of Zafar, but luckily the next morning an Afghan officer took over interviewing him. He released Zafar and advised him to keep his big mouth shut. Zafar had been lucky but obviously it had been a very stressful experience.

Now Zafar's health had improved he was desperate to find a job, and a friend told him that there was a vacancy for an English interpreter at the Palestinian Embassy. Zafar immediately applied for the post and within a week he was interviewed and offered the job. The wages were excellent and the work easy. Zafar managed to build up a close relationship with the ambassador and it seemed that that he trusted Zafar a good deal, appointing staff on Zafar's recommendation. He invited us to his house on several occasions and every time we went he gave presents to the children. When he went away, he left Zafar to take care of the embassy finances.

For a while all went well, but then dark clouds began to gather over us again. When the ambassador returned from holiday he found a large sum of money had disappeared from the office safe. The police were immediately called and within a few hours Zafar was imprisoned for suspected theft. Zafar of course protested his innocence.

Later he told me that he believed he knew who was responsible. He had begun to write against the regime again. He did not do this from home because he knew I was very unhappy about it, but used to write while he was at the embassy. There was a student named Jamal, working part-time in the embassy. He was going on holiday to Palestine and Zafar asked him if he could take some of his articles with him to post to a newspaper in America. Jamal seemed to him very trustworthy. The government had a very good relationship with Palestine, so Palestinians were unlikely to be searched at the airport. However, somehow the articles got into the hands of the Palestinian government and were sent back to the embassy for the ambassador to take action against Zafar. Zafar believed that in fact the ambassador had taken the money himself and had blamed Zafar, knowing that Zafar would not speak against him because otherwise the ambassador might hand him over to a worse fate with the *Khad*.

I was brought the news of Zafar's imprisonment by our servant, as I was teaching my class. It was a terrible shock to me. In Afghan society it is not considered proper for a woman to visit a prison but I had no option. I had to visit Zafar, so I immediately went home, collected some of his clothes, a bed sheet and a blanket and went to the prison. I was convinced that there had been some sort of misunderstanding and that the police would sort it out. I had no doubt that Zafar was innocent and wondered who had incriminated him.

The prison had an imposing gate, dirty windows,

sullen guards and a miserable crowd outside. Before I reached the main gate I saw a police officer in the courtyard. I introduced myself and asked if I could see Zafar.

'Oh that fat man who came this morning!' he said.

'Yes,' I replied.

He walked towards the gate which had a small window fitted with iron bars and spoke to someone on the other side. Then he came back and told me Zafar was not allowed out. However, if I wished to go inside I could use the office but I could not stay longer than ten minutes.

I heard the click of the padlock as I entered the prison. A guard with a gun escorted me along the long, filthy corridor which stank of urine. For a moment I thought I would suffocate. A door was opened and I was shown into a tiny, damp office to wait for Zafar. There was just one small window in the room and no curtains or carpet. There were two dusty tables scattered with papers and a few chairs. A bald man was sitting at a table playing with his fingers. He looked like a prisoner but in fact was an officer. A young lady was busy typing; she did not even bother to look at me. It seemed an eternity before Zafar appeared and, although he tried to put on a brave front for me, I was not taken in. I felt horrified seeing him under these circumstances and wondered how he would survive. He told me not to worry too much. 'The head of the innocent may go as far as the guillotine but it will not go under it,' he said. 'I am innocent and the police will sort it out soon.' He had to survive in a windowless cell which he shared with five other prisoners. Feeling totally helpless to do anything about his terrible situation, I gave him his things and went home.

Then I began my long struggle to get justice for my husband. I went from office to office but I often spoke to the wrong people who gave me bad advice. The government itself was in chaos. The change in regime meant changes in staff, so many people were new in their posts and did not know what they were doing. No one knew for sure how secure their jobs were or who could be trusted. I bribed any number of people who promised help, but three months passed and I got nowhere. I hired a lawyer who asked me for an extortionate amount in payment. I refused and employed a second lawyer who was unable to achieve anything. Then I found a third who seemed more promising. I was very relieved that he agreed to take the case as I had heard that he was a friend of the Minister of the Interior who was responsible for law and order and, even if he was not a good lawyer, I thought this friendship might help Zafar's case.

It was at this time that the authorities moved Zafar to a part of the prison reserved for long-term prisoners. This made me feel even more despondent. I felt so alone. Nobody from Zafar's family was able to help me. By this time many of them had fled

Zafar in prison

Afghanistan. My father was old and did not approve of me visiting the prison. He felt that it was not part of the Afghan tradition for a woman to be going to a male prison. My sister and brother did not have enough knowledge of the system to be able to help me. My children were too young to help. I knew that Zafar's mental state was beginning to deteriorate again, although this probably was not noticeable to others at this stage. I used to visit him every day after work and tried to give him hope but I think he knew it was false.

At that time I was only allowed to take the children to visit Zafar at certain times. Zafar's birthday was on 19 September, and Parissa insisted that we should all go to see her father in the prison, even though it was not our regular meeting day. I bought a birthday cake to take to him. However, I was not sure if the prison officer would permit this special visit and in fact we were refused. The children were very upset and Parissa started weeping. From previous visits we knew which was Zafar's room and we had marked his tiny window from outside. We slowly walked towards the backyard of the prison and stood under his window. Then the children started singing a birthday song. Zafar could hear them but we could not see him and he could not see us, as the window was too high and was built just to let light in, not to allow the prisoners to see outside. Parissa still remembers how emotional she felt as we sang outside the prison.

I remember that there was a soldier on duty by the barbed wire in front of the prison. He was jostled by the crowds of people who clamoured to see relatives and friends, and he would shout to the prisoners inside the gate that they had a visitor. He never called them solely by their names, but also by the crime they were accused of. One man was accused of being a homosexual which is illegal in Afghanistan and when the soldier called out 'Sher Ali, *bachabaaz*, the gay man', the whole crowd laughed. This must have been painful for the poor man. One day he called for Zafar, the embezzler, and again everybody laughed. This upset me very much and I could not hold back my tears, but Zafar came out and laughed loudly telling me not to upset myself. However, the next time I went, the soldier called Zafar *'bey-khar'*, which means 'couldn't care less'. It occurred to me that Zafar had probably asked him not to call him by his crime while I was there, so as not to distress me any further.

When I visited the prison, I tried to avoid getting involved in the pushing and shoving in the queue outside the gate which sometimes resulted in violence. The governor was a very serious man with a sullen face, a dark bushy moustache and a very rough look which created terror in everyone's heart. I suppose such an environment required someone like him to exert control. One day when I was standing away from the queue, I must have caught his attention. I was very scared when he came towards me, but he spoke politely and asked, 'Who do you want to see, *hamsherra* (sister)?' I think he was sympathetic to me because I was the only woman visitor. I told him that I had come to see my husband and he then asked why I was not standing in the queue. I explained that I did not feel comfortable there. He then said that Zafar seemed a very well-educated man and he wondered how he had got into such an awful situation. I replied that Zafar was innocent and I would fight for him. Then he asked me about my job and my children. I saw genuine sympathy in his eyes and knew that, despite his sullen face, he had a compassionate heart.

'Would you prefer to see Zafar in my secretary's office?' he said. I was very pleased and from then on was the only person to have the privilege of sitting in the secretary's office to wait for my husband. I still feel great gratitude towards that prison governor.

As time passed, Zafar's behaviour became more and more erratic. Sometimes he was aware of his situation and would pace up and down nervously. At other times he seemed completely unaware that he was in prison and would talk and laugh as if he was completely free. The prison officer kindly allowed Zafar to come home under police guard every two weeks to have a bath because in prison there were no facilities to wash properly. Zafar was always very generous, and on his way back to prison he would spend some of the money I gave him on food for the prisoners. I knew he was not himself because he insisted on buying tinned food for them, but this was a complete waste of money because in Afghanistan tinned food was never eaten, even in prison. We always ate fresh food and vegetables. Tinned food was imported just for the Russians.

Zafar's mental illness became obvious to everyone. He was not sleeping and was talking to himself a lot. One day a prisoner called him 'rafiq Zafar', meaning comrade. This word had recently been adopted on the Russian model by members of the communist party to replace the word 'brother', but to people who did not support the party, it was an insult. The prisoner had only used the term as a joke, but Zafar started shouting and screaming at the poor man. This convinced the prison authorities that he was very sick.

Once again he was admitted to a mental hospital and this time he had two guards standing by his bed day and night. At the beginning he had his own room, but later he was transferred to a ward with lots of other disturbed patients. Zafar stayed in the hospital for thirty days, and when he had been calmed down by the medication, he was then sent back to prison. He was given a single room which was an improvement as he was still not well.

There was another setback in my efforts to free my husband. The third lawyer who had seemed so promising told me that, though he believed in Zafar's innocence, there was nothing more he could do. He said that it was impossible to represent an individual against an embassy, which was like a government in itself. He had been my last hope. I felt completely alone with no one to lean on, wondering how it was that ordinary people like me got caught up in these extraordinary situations.

I could not go on the way I was. I had to do some-thing, so I decided to write to the Minister of the Interior myself to plead for Zafar's innocence. I had nothing to lose. The letter started to take shape in my mind and I began to put my thoughts down on paper. What I wrote was a personal appeal for justice, which came straight from my heart. When the letter was finished I wanted to hand it over personally to the minister but it was not possible to see him without an appointment. I had to go through his secretary. It was standard under the communist regime to search anyone entering a public building – something I hated. As I made my way towards the entry point, the lady responsible for the search asked if I had a weapon. I found this quite amusing and said jokingly 'yes' and put my nail file on the table. I was obviously not being sufficiently respectful considering the political climate of the time and she became very aggressive. People started to come out of their offices and I realized how stupid I had been. I quickly left the office, realizing I should have kept my feelings to myself.

When I went back, there was another person doing the searches and I entered with no problem. This time I offered the secretary a bribe to hand my letter to the minister. He refused to take the money but eventually took my letter. He promised nothing but at least it gave me something to hope for.

A week passed and there was no news. I had just convinced myself that my letter had not reached the minister when I had a phone call from the secretary giving me an appointment to see him. My heart was full of relief and hope. The following week I was shown into his office, where he was sitting at the corner of a huge table. He told me that he knew Zafar as a well-known journalist and would look into his case. I was to come back in two weeks. I thanked him, my voice shaking with nervousness. The first thing I did was to rush to the prison to give Zafar the good news but my spirits fell when I found he was tranquil-lized and did not even want to listen to me.

I remembered that when I was young my grand-mother would recite a *khatm* if she had a problem. I began to pray in the same way. Two weeks passed and I returned to the minister's office. This time I found his manner softer than before and he was easier to talk to. He told me that he had read Zafar's case and believed he was innocent. He said it was not within his power to order an immediate release but that he would speak to the ambassador in person. The case would have to come to court and Zafar would have to defend himself.

I knew Zafar was in no state to defend himself at that time, but I said nothing. I never did find out what enquiries the minister made or how he dealt with the ambassador, but I received a letter informing me that the hearing was to take place in the court next door to the prison.

Zafar had a good friend, Abdulhaq Walah, editor of the *Caravan* newspaper. He had been our tutor at university and Zafar had a high regard for him. I asked him to come and give Zafar moral support in court and he kindly agreed, but the judge refused to allow him into the court room. This meant that Zafar had nobody to support him apart from me. The court room was small, cold and silent. There were about ten people in the room and it was not clear who they were, but I did not think there were any from the Palestinian Embassy. The judge was sitting in a large chair apart from the other people, one of whom stood up and began reading the case against Zafar. When he had finished, I was relieved that there were no questions for Zafar to answer. Then it was Zafar's turn to speak. He just had to read the defence which had been prepared for him by his lawyer. Zafar was shaking and moving from one foot to another in obvious distress and I began to doubt that he could even complete this simple task. He began to read but after a few sentences made no sense and began laughing loudly. Everyone could see that he was out of control.

I could not bear to see that our opportunity to clear his name was slipping away. I stood up and asked if anyone had any objection to me reading it for him. The judge gave it some thought and asked if those present would agree to my request. Fortunately everyone did, so I took the paper from Zafar's hand and told him to sit down. It was an unusual situation as I was the only woman in the court and may have been the first woman to represent her husband. In spite of the coldness, I was covered in sweat, and somehow managed to make the sounds come out of my mouth as my heart beat faster and faster.

Slowly I began to read the paper which I had not set eyes on before. I could feel my voice echoing in the deadly silence of the court room, and I knew that all eyes were on my burning face. I do not remember what I read, but I know that the legal wording was unfamiliar. Zafar was sitting next to me and would occasionally stand up and sit down again which was very distracting. I was sure that nothing I read was registering in his troubled mind. He was playing with his fingers like a child.

When I had finished I was exhausted and felt quite faint, needing a glass of water and some fresh air. We were given a fifteen minute break and then we went back into the court room. As I took my place next to Zafar, someone whispered, 'You are a brave woman and I admire your courage in helping your husband.' I thanked him but thought how much I would prefer to live a quiet life like an ordinary woman. We waited for a long time and then the judge declared Zafar innocent. I could not believe what I was hearing. In my heart I felt such gratitude to the Minister of the Interior. Zafar was innocent but it had taken me eight long months to prove it. We went home. I was very tired and Zafar was restless. We had paid a very high price – for what? Life seemed very hard at that moment.

Chapter Five
Escape to Pakistan

My mind is raided by my thoughts
As I am an expert in sleepless nights
I try to run away from myself
With no success
Like a nightmare stuck in one place
I confront myself again and again
Like a blindfolded horse in a circle
Nothing has changed
Life is bleak

Zafar's health improved now that he was out of prison. He found a job as an interpreter at the Libyan Embassy, where he had worked previously. There was a new minister in power who was unaware of Zafar's refusal to work for the communists, so the ambassador was happy to employ him again. However, we both knew that he and the rest of the family were not safe under the communist regime. We now had three children, as I had given birth to a baby boy, Sulaiman, in 1982. Yama was now aged fourteen, Parissa ten and Sulaiman just five months old and I feared for their safety.

One night I woke up at eleven o'clock to find Zafar sitting in an armchair near our bed, deep in thought. This in itself was not unusual as there had been many sleepless nights lately, but this time I sensed that something was seriously wrong. I sat on the edge of the bed and looked closely at the face I knew so well. He seemed to have aged ten years in one night.

'They're after me again,' he explained. 'If I don't move quickly, I'll end up in prison or probably even get killed this time,' he said.

He told me that a friend who worked for the Communist Intelligence Service had warned him that the *Khad* had got hold of a copy of a broadsheet he had written denouncing the government and strongly criticizing the regime. He had gone to some lengths to explain the harsh realities of living in a communist state, and to make the public aware of what life under the puppet government was really like. This was explosive material and Zafar was in great danger. Apparently it had been retrieved from the dustbin in the office of the Libyan Embassy where Zafar worked, by a cleaning lady who was also an agent of the *Khad*. I was furious at Zafar's carelessness.

There was no time to lose. Zafar realized he had no choice but to escape to Pakistan immediately and had already made the necessary arrangements to be smuggled out. I had found him sitting there in the middle of the night trying to find a way to explain his actions to his family.

I had tears in my eyes. My world was falling apart. Confused and worried I tried to understand what was happening, but there was just too much for me to take in. A desperate panic rose up inside me. What would happen to us while he was gone?

I woke up Yama and Parissa. Sulaiman was fast asleep sensing none of my anguish. Being woken up in the middle of the night was no surprise to my two older children, as they had been aware of the dangerous situation since the beginning of the invasion, but this was different. This time their father was leaving, and they were very frightened. They bombarded him with questions. 'Where are you going? Why are you going? When will you be back? What shall we do without you?' Zafar reassured them as best he could, but he did not tell them where he was going. He stressed that they must keep absolutely quiet about his escape and not breathe a word even to the servants. That night we all lay down in my bed together. I was crying, and I could see the fear in the eyes of my two older children. They were hurt that their father was leaving us and desperately frightened, and so was I. This was the hardest part to bear of my already eventful life.

On 6 March 1983 Zafar left his family, his home and his country forever. He shaved off his beard and moustache and put on traditional Afghan clothes instead of his usual Western style. He took nothing with him except a little money. Early in the morning when the curfew broke, he left us. I stood near our big iron gate watching him move slowly away from me, wondering if I would ever see him again. Then he was gone.

The real nightmare started for me once Zafar had left. The future was unpredictable and dark. I was numb with fear, confused and alone, without anyone to help me. What would happen if I could not convince the authorities that Zafar was just missing? What if they were to find out he had escaped? What if he were caught during his journey over the mountains to Pakistan? And most frightening of all, what if they were to take my son Yama instead of Zafar?

At that time the *Khad* had no qualms about holding hostage the sons of dissidents. I had a colleague, a teacher like myself, whose husband lost his job because he did not co-operate with the regime. He fled to America intending that the family should join him there as soon as they could. Tragically someone reported his escape and the *Khad* imprisoned his eldest son who was only fourteen years old in his place. After a month his father returned and was able to save his son's life but it cost him his own.

Zafar and I had planned how we would handle his 'disappearance'. I would wait for two days before taking any action. The two days passed slowly and I was in agony with anxiety. Then, with my heart in my mouth, I went to the police and reported that my husband was missing. I sensed their suspicion, but I must have been in a very bad state because they seemed to feel sorry for me. They assured me that they would do anything they could to help, but I knew this was unlikely because the city was in such turmoil that even the police were overwhelmed with their own fears and problems.

Then I had news from the secretary at the Libyan Embassy, who was a very close friend of Zafar's, that he had arrived safely in Pakistan. The relief was tremendous. I made some *halwa* and sent it to the local mosque, as I had vowed to God that I would. It was a miracle the *Khad* had not bothered us. Maybe they did search for Zafar, but by this time it was too late. I knew God was on my side and after two weeks of anxiety things began to return almost to normal, and for a while I heard nothing more.

Day followed night and night followed day. To all outward appearances we were leading a normal life, but in reality I was busy planning a way for us to leave the country without attracting attention. I emphasized the importance of secrecy to my children and warned them to say nothing, not even to the servants. They understood the risks we were taking and kept quiet. I decided that New Year's Eve was the best possible time for us to escape, as it would not arouse suspicion if we were away from home. I told the servants we were going to visit my brother, Sayed Taleb Shah, and my father who lived with my brother and his family. I said we would be staying there overnight.

That afternoon I was very emotional. I felt as if something inside me had died. I was about to leave the home I had lived in for fifteen years, which held a lifetime of shared memories, problems, pains and joys. It was a quiet and peaceful afternoon. I wandered from room to room, looking around carefully. I knew I needed to remember every minute detail as I was not allowed to take anything with me and I would never see this house again. I did not cry for what I felt was something beyond tears.

At five o'clock in the afternoon of 21 March 1983 we left the security of our home for an unknown future. I wanted to say a proper farewell to my maid and her family, to put my arms round them and tell them I would not see them again, but I could not. I just had to say a casual goodbye, as if we were going on a normal New Year's visit to my brother's house and would return the next day. My heart was breaking. As the taxi took us to my brother's house, I stared hard at everything around me – the beautiful blue sky, the trees, the plants, even the roads and the shops. They all looked different to me. It was as though I had never really looked at them before. Suddenly everything was very precious and I felt very emotional.

That night in my brother's house everyone was upset. My father was inconsolable and all he managed to say was just the one sentence.

'I shall never see you again,' he said.

'Don't say that,' I begged. 'You will. I will be back

and we will all be together.'

Early the following day we tearfully hugged and kissed each other and said our goodbyes. My sister-in-law Shereen held the Holy Quran over our heads as we stepped out of the house. My Aunt Zainab had come to see us off, and there were tears streaming down her cheeks. She threw a bucket of water behind us which traditionally means that the person will soon be back. It was then that I realized how much I would miss them. I did not look back as I knew my father would be crying and I did not want to see his tears. When we were out of sight I let myself weep bitterly.

Two years later my brother Sayed Taleb Shah wrote to say that my father had passed away. Sadly my father had been right – we did not see each other again. My brothers, unable to endure the endless fighting in Afghanistan, escaped with their families to Pakistan after my father died. Sayed Taleb Shah and his family managed to escape to Canada where they are still living, while my elder brother, Sayed Shah, returned to Afghanistan after the fall of the Taliban in 2002.

We had made arrangements to meet our two guides at the bus stop. They were distant relatives of Zafar's but we were to show no signs of recognition. They sat at the back of the bus while the three children and I stayed at the front. We were all dressed like nomads and my face was covered in a veil. We had been advised to speak to no one. As the bus drew away, I had to restrain myself from waving to my brother who was watching from a distance. Tears were burning my face as the bus moved away. I saw my brother getting smaller and smaller and mouthed silently, 'God be with you'. My eldest son, Yama, was desperately worried to see me so upset and also terrified that we might be discovered. Parissa who was younger was not so aware of the great danger we were in and saw it as an adventure. Sulaiman, the baby, was still being breast-fed and had no idea about what was happening.

The bus set off for the east, heading for Jalalabad, a big city near the Pakistan border. As we journeyed into our unknown future my mind wandered back over my former life in Kabul, my family and friends, people whose tragedies we had shared. I remembered another night two years previously when two drunk Russian soldiers had forced their way into our house. Zafar and I were terrified and quickly hid the children in the wardrobe and under the bed. My brother-in-law rushed out of the room to see what the soldiers would do. When the soldiers asked for money we gave them some and managed to get rid of them. As we pulled the children out from their hiding places, I thanked God for saving us. We could so easily have been killed.

Other friends were not so fortunate. One friend, the wife of a senator, was raped in front of three of her children. Then they were all killed. Her husband was away at the time and her remaining son, a boy of fourteen, hid in the yard, but ten months later, unable to cope with the memory, he committed suicide. When we visited the senator, I could see in his eyes something far beyond rage, pain or sorrow, something you would never be able to explain. The catastrophe of losing his family had totally destroyed him.

I also thought of my friend Sarah, and how we had been unable to weep at the funeral of her uncle. Many other members of her family had been in the notorious Pull-e-Churki prison because of their wealthy background and refusal to co-operate with the current regime. When Babrak Karmal came to power, two of her brothers were released but there was no trace of her father. It was as though he had never existed.

Suddenly the bus came to a halt and I was jolted back into the present and the dangers we all faced. Two soldiers from the military station climbed on board to search the bus and their suspicious eyes made me sweat and shiver under my veil. I started praying, 'Dear God, please don't let them find us out.' Parissa and Yama's faces were very white. The soldiers asked us to stand up and they looked under our seats, but they did not say anything. They got off the bus and allowed us to move on. We were able to breathe normally again.

The journey was slow as the roads were damaged from mortar shells and mines. Once again our bus was stopped, but fortunately this time it was for two tired young Russian soldiers who just wanted a ride. It should have taken three hours to reach Jalalabad and it took us nine, but eventually we reached our destination. It was late afternoon when we arrived, exhausted. Our guides were very relieved that the first stage of the journey was over. For them it was the hardest part because there were a lot of soldiers between Kabul and Jalalabad, and they had no wish to be confronted by the military. They took us to a dilapidated house where we stayed for two weeks until it was considered safe for us to move on. The family who lived there provided us with everything we needed, as we could not go outside at all.

Amazingly, we found my husband's aunt there with her entire family. They had arrived two days before from Kabul and were also fleeing to Pakistan. Their presence gave us moral support but their situation was different from ours, as they originally came from Jalalabad and spoke Pashto, the language also spoken in Peshawar in Pakistan. This meant it would be easier for them to get over the border provided they found a soldier to bribe, which eventually they managed to do. Our situation was much more difficult, as we did not speak Pashto and had fair complexions and round faces, unlike the local people. It was impossible for us to get across the border, so we would have to take the difficult route over the mountains.

I was then faced with a very difficult decision. The guides suggested that I allow Parissa to cross the border with Zafar's aunt and her family, as it would save her the harsh journey over the mountains which they thought she might not manage. They were planning to travel by road over the Khyber Pass, whereas we would be going by an even more moun-tainous route, and would have to climb on foot for much of the way. Parissa had a rather darker com-plexion than the rest of us, so could pass as one of the local people.

Parissa was quite happy to go with the others and saw it as another part of this great adventure. She loved the mountains and was too young to be aware of the danger that we might be split up and never see each other again. Reluctantly I agreed. I believed she would be safe with Zafar's aunt and his family, and would reach her father sooner, but the thought of parting with her gave me sleepless nights. However, I consoled myself with the knowledge that it was for her own good.

The family split into three groups as they could not all go at once. Parissa was in the first group of three, which consisted of another girl of twelve and a boy aged sixteen, who was full of self confidence. Two or three days before they left, we bought the girls long, black *kochi* (dresses worn by local nomad women) and big, blanket-like *chader* (pieces of material which cover the whole body from head to toe). They were not allowed to change their clothes or even wash their faces, so they would look like the local children who sometimes crossed the border between Afghanistan and Pakistan, doing some kind of small business between Jalalabad and Peshawar to support their families. Sometimes, the checkpoint soldiers were kind enough to let them through, but things were quite different with children from Kabul who were likely to be imprisoned.

Parissa's companions taught her a few words of Pashto in case of an emergency. Otherwise she was told to keep silent during the journey. After they had left for the coach station I started to panic, thinking how foolish I had been to let my young daughter be parted from me. I kept blaming myself over and over again. What if she fell sick? What if we could not get through this journey and were sent back to Kabul or put in prison and I lost my daughter forever? I had so many questions in my mind, but it was too late – she had gone. Suddenly there was a knock at the door and my heart sank. We all rushed to see who it was and then amazingly I heard Parissa's laughter. I thought I was going mad. Then I saw her, with her two companions, laughing and repeating the Pashto words she had been taught a few days ago. I was overwhelmed with relief and vowed I would never let her go without me again.

Then the three young people told us their story. Long before they reached the border, the coach had been stopped at a military checkpoint. Everybody was asked for their travel documents and why they were going to Pakistan. When it was Parissa's cousin's turn, she lost her tongue but Parissa answered *'Gandi – Ca voom'* (we're doing some business). Apparently the officer laughed. 'Good plan,' he said, 'but do you think I was born yesterday? You dressed the part very well but your stupid parents forgot to change your expensive shoes. Do you think nomad girls wear shoes like you? You are lucky I'm not going to send you to prison. Go back to your brainless parents who put your life at risk. If I ever see you again, I will know what to do with you.' So they got off the bus and walked back to the house where we were staying. That night I slept well, but I could not help wondering what would have happened if the officer had reacted differently.

After two long and isolated weeks Yama, Parissa, Sulaiman and I began the next stage of our journey, led by our guides. First, we travelled to the village of Besoud where we stayed in the house of Ustad Asif. This small village was located in one of the most beautiful parts of the world. The grass lay like green velvet before us, the sky was a clear blue, and the trees were covered in blossom. If circumstances had been different we would all have enjoyed our time there. The house where we stayed was big and divided into two compounds, one for the women and children and another for the men. Yama, who was now fourteen, went to the men's compound while the rest of us stayed with the women. Everybody was so kind and hospitable to us. The people there led a very simple rural life, far from the city's turmoil. Modern technology had not reached Besoud and there were no telephones or televisions. Men and women accepted their traditional roles in life and the desire for equality between the sexes did not exist. The people demanded no more than to live in content-ment with their donkeys, hens and sheep. Their happy and contented faces seemed to me to be honest and straightforward, and I could have lived in such a quiet and peaceful atmosphere forever. Sadly, that beautiful village has since been bombed and no one lives there any more.

Early next morning after a hurried breakfast, we left the village. I carried Sulaiman, as our guides led the way through the fields for more than an hour until we reached a dusty road. It was still only six o'clock when we saw a large open lorry with neither roof nor sides waiting for us. The only seats were in the front and were for the driver and our two lucky guides. In the back of the lorry were sacks of wheat and also four nomad families, including women and children. We were the only fugitives among them and were warned not to speak because our accents would give us away.

We climbed onto the lorry and settled ourselves on top of the sacks of wheat. Iron rails had been put up as makeshift sides around us, but the sacks felt unstable and we were very uncomfortable. The engine started and we moved off through a constant cloud of dust. As the lorry wound its way through the mountains, the tiny road became even narrower and my discomfort turned to panic. The aged engine seemed to overheat every few miles, as we climbed the steep gradients. Every time it overheated, we had to stop while the men threw water over the engine to cool it down. Eventually, by fits and starts we reached the mountain peak from where the houses and villages below looked like tiny match boxes. I heard someone whisper that down below in the gorge was a lorry which had slipped the previous year and twenty people had died. I was terrified, and started crying under my veil as we continued on our way. We were high up in the mountains on an ancient lorry whose wheels were inches away from a drop of several thousand feet, and by the time we stopped again I was numb with fear.

We all assumed that the engine needed to cool down, but then the driver told us that because of the recent rainfall a large part of the narrow road had been washed over the edge, making it impossible to go any further for the moment. All the men were looking for a large enough rock to fill the hole and repair the road. This was the last straw as far as I was concerned. I felt that our lives were being risked too casually. I could imagine my children tumbling into the dark, fast-flowing river roaring away thousands of feet below and I went crazy. I began to shout and scream and became quite hysterical, cursing the current regime for creating this desperate situation. The children were very embarrassed as we had been told to keep silent so as not to give ourselves away by our accents. I grabbed them and started to run through the mountains not knowing where I was going.

This show of hysteria must have frightened my poor children and it also disturbed everyone else, including our guides. They let me go for a while and then the driver, who was a compassionate man, came after me and calmed me down promising to drive very carefully. When the road was repaired we all climbed back on board the lorry but I felt as if I was already dead. I felt sure we were not going to come out of this journey alive. The guides made sure I sat on the mountain side and did not look over the edge, while they talked to me all the time to take my mind off my fears and tried their best to make the rest of the journey bearable if not comfortable.

It was late evening when we finally arrived at the foot of the mountain. There was still a long way to go, but at least we were on level ground. We eventually reached a village. It was pitch dark with only the stars to light the sky, and the building before us resembled a haunted house surrounded by high walls and towering trees. Then we went through a huge wooden gate and our guides knocked on the door, which immediately set the dogs barking. From inside came a voice asking us to identify ourselves.

'We are strangers from Kabul and have no place to stay for the night. We need help,' our guides replied.

The door opened very cautiously, but when the man behind it saw there was a woman and children in the group his attitude changed. He ushered us through a big, dusty yard to the *tandoor khana* (the bakery). It was dark, smoky and very warm and we all sat down gratefully on the bare floor near the oven. After having some bread to eat and a cup of tea, we all lay down on the floor to sleep, happy to have found somewhere to rest. In the morning light the house did not look so intimidating. The guides offered our host some money but he refused, saying that guests are a gift from God.

At this point the lorry turned back as there was no road from here on. We knew we would either have to walk or hire animals to ride. Our guides went into the village to see if they could hire any horses or donkeys, but there were none available until the following day. We decided not to wait and after a small breakfast we set off on foot through the mountains. I was quite happy as I disliked riding animals and, looking at what lay ahead of us, I felt it would be safer on foot. For the first three or four hours we walked up the foothills and then began the slow climb up the high mountain from where the views were breathtaking. The guides took it in turns to carry Sulaiman for me. There was one terrible moment when I looked back and saw that one of the guides had stumbled and dropped him. The guide rushed to pick Sulaiman up and luckily he was so well protected by a thick blanket that he came to no harm.

After the dreadful experience of the day before, the climb was almost pleasant. There were times when I thought I would go mad with frustration and exhaustion but there were also times when the beauty of nature, the grandeur of the mountains and the freshness of the wild plains made me light-headed with exhilaration.

When we reached the top of the mountain, the whirring of helicopters in the distance quickly restored my sense of reality. I had no idea of the danger we were in until our guides signalled to us to scatter and hide behind the rocks and bushes. If we had been spotted there is little doubt we would have been killed. A chill went through my spine and my heart started to pound as I rushed towards the bushes carrying my baby son, my eyes searching for my other two children. One of my plastic slippers came off and disappeared down the mountain but I did not care. I threw myself behind a large bush and ducked down, covering Sulaiman, closing my eyes and praying that Yama and Parissa were safely hidden. The helicopters were roaring towards us and I thought it was the end. I gave my family and myself into the care of God and my mind seemed to go completely blank as the helicopters came nearer and nearer, passed directly over our heads and then went on, eventually disappearing from sight. By this time I was numb with shock.

We did not move from our hiding places until the guides decided that the danger had passed. Then we struggled up from behind the bushes and hugged each other with relief, ready to continue our journey. Although I was now barefoot it did not matter because we were alive. As we kept walking, the weather changed and became very cold. The wind started to blow and the guides tied Sulaiman onto my back for safety. The path was very narrow, but now we were going down the mountain progress was much easier.

It was almost midnight when we reached level ground. We sat down near a tiny outbuilding on the foothills where the air was still and silent and the darkness of this remote, unknown place overpowering. The guides hoped we could get some food and shelter in the nearby village but I did not really care. I was so exhausted by then that I just wanted to lie down and never wake up again, but I knew I had to go on. The children, who had managed the arduous journey amazingly well, were also exhausted by this time.

One of the guides went down to the village and came back with a man holding a lantern. He said it was not possible to provide us with a room because it was too late, but that we could shelter in his stable. We had no alternative but to accept. Then someone brought us some tea and bread and we felt a little better. At first it was difficult for our eyes to adjust to the darkness, but gradually we got used to it. Three filthy beds were dragged in for the children and me, but the two guides slept on the rough floor, their hands under their heads. Everyone else seemed to sleep but I couldn't. I heard deep snoring around me. My throat tightened with a deep sadness and my eyes were burning. I asked myself, was not this too much to pay for other people's mistakes?

Early next morning we faced the prospect of another long journey through the mountains. We had not been able to wash for three days, but I knew there was no point in asking for water so we put up with it. The guides managed to hire three donkeys and a driver, who was paid to accompany us to the next stage of our journey. I climbed onto my poor donkey which I remember had a large wound on its back. The guides tied Sulaiman to my lap with some cloth. By this time I had no shoes and my face had to be covered with a veil which I was only allowed to remove when we were in the mountains. Eventually, we reached a deep gorge full of thorny plants and shrubs, and as we rode the thorns tore at my bare feet, but I was unable to move around on the donkey and so was not able to help myself. To make matters worse our progress was pathetically slow because of the thick plant growth we had to negotiate as we passed through the gorge.

Unexpectedly, we heard the sound of shooting

nearby. Our guides rushed to help me down from the donkey and shouted at the children to hide under the bushes. Terrified we dismounted and hid ourselves as the bullets poured down from above. From our cover we could hear shooting for several minutes and then it died away, and we were able to emerge from our hiding places. I remember thinking to myself that things like that only happen in the movies, but this was all too real.

It was late afternoon when we were allowed to have a rest, and we all sat down for a simple meal of bread, cheese and water. The driver and his donkeys turned back here and once again we started to walk, but there was a new horror ahead. We had to cross a wide river. Fortunately, it was not as deep as we had expected but it was running very fast. When we first waded in, we were able to jump carefully from stone to stone in the shallow water but then the water got deeper and reached our waists. One of the guides carried Sulaiman so that it was easier for me to cross but half-way through he slipped and dropped my son. I closed my eyes in horror and truly thought I would go mad, but he grabbed him quickly and when I looked again Sulaiman had started crying loudly. It was such a relief to see he was alright. After what seemed an age in the freezing water we clambered out onto the bank. The sun had gone in and we were very cold, so we moved on quickly to the next village where we found shelter with a very hospitable family, who gave us food and fairly clean beds. I was overjoyed when one of our guides said that our journey was nearly at an end and we should be in Pakistan by the following evening. At last! This was something I had been longing to hear for three days. After a good rest we resumed our journey the next morning and about one o'clock sat down to eat the boiled eggs our hosts had kindly provided for us.

In the distance we could see a crowd of people with their donkeys, camels and trucks. We had no idea why they had congregated in that particular spot but were delighted to discover that one of our enter- prising guides had negotiated a lift for us on one of the trucks. At least we were delighted until we saw the vehicle. The reality was far worse than walking or riding on a donkey as the tiny truck was only about two by three square metres and had no sides at all. It was like a board on four wheels and there were approximately twenty to thirty passengers. We all climbed on in a great rush to sit near the middle, perching on each others' shoulders, laps and knees. Half my body disappeared under other people's legs, arms and hands and I was so cramped that it was impossible to breast feed Sulaiman. We were all loaded on the truck like dead animals, and a strong rope was passed round the outside to hold us in. We moved slowly as there was no road, just wet muddy earth. Yama was sitting near a wheel and, as it turned, the mud flew straight into his face. He could not do anything about it as he had to hold onto the rope with both hands for his own safety, so by the end of three hours his face looked like a blob of wet earth and his eyes were completely closed. We could not move our bodies except for our necks, but we kept reminding each other that it was the last part of the journey. Looking back, I don't know how, but sometimes, we even managed to laugh.

After three long hours of hardship, the truck came to a halt and the guides who had been sitting comfortably inside the cabin came to untie the rope. They announced proudly that we were almost in Pakistan, except for one thing. We still had to climb the great mountain in front of us. We were already stiff from the truck ride and now had to face the exhausting climb ahead. The rain was pouring down as we struggled along, and ended up literally crawling on our hands and knees. By the time we reached the top we were soaked to the skin but overjoyed that below us lay Pakistan and freedom. I looked back for the last time at my beautiful homeland which I will never forget, the country where I had belonged. I felt like a small bird with broken wings, who would never be able to fly again. Tears rolled down my cheeks and mixed with the rain. I thought the sky was crying too for this fugitive woman with her three young children, who had come to find a new country for themselves. Then we climbed down the mountain and were in Pakistan.

Chapter Six
Pakistan

A winter tree without leaves
A wingless bird that cannot fly
A silent weep without tears
The tree, the bird and the tears
Grow together
Year after year

At the foot of the mountain which divides Afghanistan and Pakistan we found a bus waiting and eagerly climbed on board. This bus was for those fleeing from Afghanistan and had been arranged by the people who regularly smuggled desperate human cargo over the border illegally. There were twenty of us in all, none of us with any travel documents. No one asked us where we were heading but I presumed we were going to Peshawar. We were just grateful to be in Pakistan and out of the pouring rain. We were soaked to the skin but as we had no change of clothes we just huddled together in silence for the next part of the journey. After four or five hours we arrived at a tiny village which had just a couple of shops and a small teahouse where we hoped to find food and rest.

Our guides ushered us into the teahouse which was divided by a filthy curtain into separate areas for men and women. All the women were herded into the back part where someone thankfully lit an oven-like open fire as we were freezing cold and shivering. After some tea and boiled eggs we began to feel slightly better. One of the guides tried unsuccessfully to buy me some shoes or slippers from the nearby shops. Even if he had found some, I probably would not have been able to get them on as my feet were bruised and swollen from walking barefoot over the mountains. We rested for about an hour and then climbed wearily onto the bus for the very last part of our journey which was to end, for the moment, in Peshawar.

Late in the evening we knocked on the door of a small flat in Peshawar belonging to one of Zafar's distant relatives who had escaped from Afghanistan a few months earlier. The relief I experienced when they opened the door and gave us a warm welcome is hard to describe. I just looked at my children and knew we were safe.

The family were extremely kind and hospitable, and I shall always remember them with gratitude. They immediately offered us a change of clothes and brought me a tub of hot, salty water to soak my wounded feet. We were given a soothing drink, a special remedy made from milk and oil, and then, most welcome of all, someone took care of Sulaiman and let me sleep. After twenty days of extreme anxiety and unimaginable fears, I slept like one already dead. The next morning we were happily reunited with Zafar. Zafar had arrived safely after coming over the same mountains as we had. He had also found the journey arduous, especially as he was a large man, not used to physical activity. He said that on the way he kept wondering how his family would ever be able to manage such a journey.

However, our troubles were by no means over. We had not brought any money with us, as it was not safe to carry it over the mountains. Before leaving Kabul I had made arrangements for our money to be brought across the border at a suitable time but, until it arrived, we had to manage without any money at all. Zafar found a place to stay in the house of a wealthy Pakistani family who were in some way related to my father-in-law. I had not met them before but had heard a great deal about their closeness to my father-in-law, and so I found it odd that they chose to keep their distance from us and never asked us to have dinner or even a cup of tea with them. Perhaps it was a part of their culture to behave like this but in Afghanistan we treated our guests differently. However, I appreciated that they could have refused to help us at all, and then we would have been in the unenviable position of having no money and nowhere to stay. Although I was very depressed at the time, I did realize that things could have been worse.

Peshawar, on the border between Afghanistan and Pakistan, was swollen with refugees, tents and makeshift shanties spreading for miles and miles. These refugees lived in squalor in the filthy, over-crowded camps where people only tried to survive. Around the camps you could see hundreds of graves, mostly of children who had died of disease or hunger and women from childbirth, while Afghan warlords built palaces with the international aid donated to help refugees in the camps. International aid went through the Pakistani government, who divided it between the different warlords who imposed their own law on the camps. The money was supposed to help refugees, but instead it went into the pockets of Pakistanis or Afghan warlords. These warlords were the leaders of the Mujahideen, who called themselves freedom fighters against the Soviet-backed regime in Afghanistan. There were seven different factions among the Mujahideen, who fought amongst them-selves as well as against their common enemy. United States policy was to support the warlords to defeat the Soviet Union, so they provided aid to train the Mujahideen.

Life under the Mujahideen was very different from in Afghanistan. Girls had no chance to go to school while the boys went to *madrassas* (religious schools) just to memorise the Quran and get brainwashed by mullahs who misinterpreted Islam. These religious schools, funded by Islamic countries, took in thousands of refugee boys from the camps and, as well as teaching them to memorize the Quran in Arabic, indoctrinated them with fundamentalist ideas that were anti-women, the west and civilization in general. Now in the twentieth century, wearing perfume was a sin, laughing with a male relative was a sin, walking alone in the street was a sin, raising a *chaderi* to expose any part of the face and body was a sin. Suddenly women had no freedom at all. Mullahs declared that women should be banned from work and should wear the veil, despite the fact that women had been active in the economic life of Afghanistan for decades. All Afghan refugee women were terrified of the Mujahideen, young men with beards, wearing turbans and carrying guns, who used Islam to assert their power over women.

We soon learnt that there was very little chance of privacy. It was vital to be very cautious especially as a woman, which was a new experience for me and totally at variance with my previous lifestyle. All Afghan women were now watched over by the Mujahideen who had full control over us. They watched how we spoke to shop keepers, how we walked in the streets, how we behaved and how we dressed. We not only had to come to terms with a new environment but also had to learn to be very cautious when dealing with the mullahs, some of whom were completely uneducated and very dogmatic. One day I was shopping with my ten-year-old daughter, Parissa, when a young Afghan Mujahid shouted at her because her *chader* had slipped down from her head down to her shoulders. He ordered her to put it back on her head and added, 'If I see you again dressed improperly I shall know what to do with you.' Parissa was ready to answer him back in anger, but I knew this would lead to trouble so I quickly intervened and said, 'You are quite right, she won't let it happen again.' After that I never let her go out without making sure her scarf was firmly secured on her head. The fear that we might run into trouble never left my heart as long as we were in that environment.

In Pakistan it was compulsory for all Afghan refugees to carry a pass or proof of nationality. To get a pass, refugees had to go to the office of the particular faction of the Mujahideen they came under. They each had separate offices and were quite hostile to those from other factions. Zafar set off to go to the offices of the Dari-speaking faction to collect our identification papers. He was wearing a Western suit although he was aware this might cause offence, but he had no choice as, without any money, he was not in a position to buy any new traditional Afghan clothes. When Zafar did not return by the evening I began to get really worried and by the next morning I was in a state of panic. I did not know what to do.

I had no friends in Peshawar and I suspected that the family who were reluctantly sheltering us would not want to get involved in a 'disappearance'. I was very surprised when an Afghan friend, Sher Zaman, called to see me as I did not even know he was in Pakistan, but he brought disturbing news. Zafar had been arrested by the Mujahideen and was in their prison. Sher Zaman did not know exactly what had happened but it appeared that Zafar had had an argument with a mullah. I felt my knees go weak as I remembered my bitter experiences at the prison in Kabul. I could not go through all that again, not here, not now. Sher Zaman urged me not to do anything for a day or two. He felt that if the case was not too serious, Zafar would be released but if it was, he would find some way to help.

For four days I heard nothing, but on the fifth day Sher Zaman returned and seemed very worried. He brought news that thirteen mullahs had issued a *fatwa* (religious decree) saying that Zafar had insulted the Prophet Mohammed. 'They are very angry,' he said. 'If you don't move quickly, something very dangerous will happen and Zafar might be killed.' I was very shocked and confused. I knew that Zafar would not have insulted the Prophet on purpose and I wondered what on earth could have happened for such a misunderstanding to have arisen.

In Kabul I had got used to the idea that every time Zafar went out he might not come back, but he would always say, 'My time is not up yet.' On this occasion I thought his time 'was up' and asked myself just how I was going to manage in a foreign country with three children. I was really angry at Zafar. How could he put us in this position? What had he done?

Sher Zaman said that he would try to get me an appointment with the leaders of the Dari-speaking faction of the Mujahideen, Sabghatullah Mujadidi. I waited for two days, all the time wondering if the leader might refuse to see me, and if he did agree to see me, what if I made the situation worse. Then I heard that he had granted me an audience. I covered myself from head to toe with a heavy cotton *chaderi,* hired a rickshaw and set off with Yama accompanying me. I was full of anxiety and my mouth was empty of words – I had no idea how to plead for Zafar's release. The weather was hot, the traffic very heavy and the young rickshaw driver none too careful – in Pakistan the rickshaw drivers have laws of their own. They keep neither to the left or the right, the music in their cabins is ear-piercing, and they shout and gesticulate at people who walk across the road in front of them. All this, together with the noise of their horns and the heat, was almost too much for me in my anxious state.

Eventually, Yama and I found ourselves standing in front of the gate of the house of the Mujahideen leader. Two guards were on duty and I spoke to them wearing my veil over my face, and with fear in my heart as I waited for their reply. They were clearly uncomfortable talking to a woman but they did allow me in, but Yama had to remain with them and I noticed that no boys appeared to be allowed to enter the house except for close family. I was ushered into a living room where there were three beautiful and courteous women who immediately made me feel more relaxed.

Tea was brought in without my asking, as is our custom. The room was decorated in typical Afghan style with a red rug in the centre surrounded by *toshak (*mattresses) covered with smaller rugs and cushions. There were no tables or chairs and the simplicity of their lifestyle was obvious. When the leader entered the room, we all rose to greet him. He was a slim man with round glasses, wearing a white turban and a white *shalwar* and *kamiz* (traditional Afghan dress). When he sat down on the corner of the *toshak,* everyone else also sat down. I explained in a trembling voice why I had come to see him. He replied that Zafar had no right to insult the Prophet Mohammed under any circumstances. It was not acceptable and we should know that.

He spoke in a very calm voice and I opened my mouth to reason with him, but quickly changed my mind for I realized that it would be pointless, as he obviously believed what the mullahs had told him. I decided to try a different approach. 'My husband has only just been released from a mental institution,' I explained. 'Under Islamic law, you can't punish a person who is mentally ill and sometimes not responsible for his actions. I apologize for his behaviour.' He asked if I had any proof from the hospital and I had to admit that I had none but I added, 'I swear to God that he was in a mental institution and in prison.' I began to weep and the ladies in the room wept with me as I told of our escape. I explained how our lives had been in danger owing to Zafar's undercover activities against the regime.

The leader listened carefully and then interrupted when he heard the name. 'This Zafar. Is he Zafar Shadji?' he asked. 'Yes, he is,' I answered quickly. There was a long pause and then he said. 'I know Zafar well. He was my cleverest student when I was teaching and I also knew his father who was a great man. I wish you had some papers from the hospital, as it would make things easier to deal with.' Saying that, he reached for a phone and ordered Zafar to be put in a private room with a fan and to be given anything he needed. He also asked for his papers to be sent to him. He put down the phone and turned back to me. 'I can't release him immediately but I will speak to the mullahs to calm the situation first, then I shall see what I can do for him.'

I was very grateful and would have kissed his hand if I had dared, but instead I asked if I could take Zafar some clothes.

'No, it might not be good for a woman to go to the prison. I will arrange something for him,' he replied.

A week later Zafar was released and at the same time our money arrived from Kabul. I asked him why he had been imprisoned and he blamed it on his beard which he said made him look like Lenin! Apparently, when he was collecting our identification it was prayer time and a mullah had asked him to join them in prayers. According to the Islamic religion, it is important to wash before praying. Zafar told them he had not washed himself and so was unclean for prayer, and would pray when he got home, but the mullah accused him of not being a good Muslim and started shouting at him. Zafar answered him back and a crowd of people gathered round, all taking the mullah's side. This was to be expected because this was the mullah's territory and Zafar should have remembered that, but he did not think. He was surrounded by mullahs and two guards took him by the shoulder and threw him into a room, locking the door behind him. Nobody had said anything against the Prophet Mohammed, but when the case reached the ear of the leader it was told differently. It was not only the Afghan women refugees in Pakistan who had to be wary of the mullahs; the men were also vulnerable.

Now that we had some money, we decided it was time to leave Peshawar and move to the capital of Pakistan, Islamabad. Islamabad was a bigger city than Peshawar and less dominated by the Mujahideen. Temperatures soared in Islamabad, sometimes reaching 45 degrees Centigrade, while in Afghanistan the maximum was 35 degrees, and it only very rarely reached this temperature. We had very little money and we arrived in Islamabad with no plan about where to stay. Zafar managed to contact an Afghan man, who kindly took us to his house. He had one large room where he lived with his family, and he divided the room into two with a curtain and we lived in one half for a week. Then we rented a small flat nearby.

One morning I found Sulaiman covered from head to foot with a rash. I took him to a doctor who said he was suffering from the heat and prescribed some medicine. I was relieved it was nothing more dangerous, but within a week we were all suffering from the same irritating itchy rash. The children were in tears, walking around with their hands on their heads for fear of exacerbating the irritation under their arms. The heat was unbearable and every few hours we had to change out of our sodden clothes which created lots of extra washing, and we were always short of things to wear. Our small two-bedroom flat had just one fan which we crowded under, eating and sleeping there with the fleas dancing around us.

On one of those burning afternoons I sent Yama to the shop to buy some yoghurt, cucumber and ice as I wanted to make a special Afghan cold drink. He came home with only the yoghurt and the cucumber. 'Where is the ice?' I asked. He showed me the jug of warm water from the melted ice and I just sat down, crying and laughing at the same time.

We decided to find an alternative place to live, so we were delighted when someone offered us the use of his summer home in Murree which is a beautiful area in the foothills of the Himalayas. Things were looking up. Zafar had been offered a job as a Dari newscaster for Radio Pakistan in Islamabad which meant he would have to stay in the capital, but at least I could move the children out of the heat and the flies which were driving us mad. But disappointment was to follow. Zafar accompanied us to Murree and when we arrived we found our accommodation only consisted of two tiny rooms which had four filthy beds in them. There was no electricity, no water, no kitchen, no chairs and no rugs. A big table stood in the middle of one room which was obviously supposed to be the cooking area. The lavatory was outside in the backyard. We unpacked our things and I started to make a home again.

The next morning Zafar went back to his job in Islamabad, and I went out to look around and hopefully find some friendly neighbours, but we were in the middle of nowhere. There were plenty of trees but no people at all. I sat down on a big rock and wondered what I was going to do in this place. What if we were attacked? But it was too late. Zafar had gone and I had to wait for him to come back which would not be for two weeks. At least we would appreciate the cooler weather. Suddenly I heard a faint sound of water trickling and was delighted to find a spring of water bubbling up from the ground. At least one problem had been solved.

When we investigated further we found that, thankfully, we were not as isolated as we had first thought. There was a small road from near our house which led to the top of the mountains where we found some shops and a tourist bazaar. We soon got used to walking up there and found another Afghan family who had also come from Islamabad to avoid the heat. We were able to be a great help to each other. We also came across a Pakistani family living in a house surrounded by tall trees about a mile away from us. The man of the house was a doctor and ran a small clinic in Murree.

When it was dark there was not much we could do without any electricity, so reluctantly we would go to bed early and I would begin the long and often sleepless night I knew would lie ahead of me. It was on such a night at about two o'clock that I awoke to find Sulaiman crying. He had an ear infection and was very upset. Suddenly he began to shiver and shake, stopped breathing and lapsed into unconsciousness. I thought he was dead. I started to scream and carried him outside. With my two other children following I ran barefoot up the mountain to the doctor's house. It was pitch black and I was not even sure we were going in the right direction. I collapsed exhausted on the ground and Yama took Sulaiman and climbed further up the mountain.

I pulled myself up and followed behind as quickly as I could, shouting, 'God, God, God! What have I done to deserve this? How long are you going to continue to torture me?' Then a voice called out from the doctor's house, as they had heard us coming. By the time we had got there Sulaiman was breathing again and was crying, so I felt the danger had passed. The doctor kindly let us all stay the night. He gave me some medicine for Sulaiman then we took him home, but the experience had really frightened me.

I waited anxiously for Zafar to arrive at the end of the two weeks but he did not turn up. I was furious with him for abandoning us, for leaving us alone and not seeming to care any more about us. In the third week he came, but we had a bitter argument and he did not stay. Then it was Yama's turn to fall sick and the doctor suggested I take him to the hospital so again I packed up all our things and we set off, this time for Rawalpindi. We had a friend there, Ahmad Shah Seddiqi from our university days, and he immediately found us a doctor who prescribed antibiotics but it was still a week before Yama could stand. When he was well, we all returned to the flat in Islamabad.

If I wrote a hundred pages about our terrible living conditions in Pakistan I still would not be able to express all the misery I felt there. We were desperate to get out of Pakistan. We applied to the American Embassy for acceptance as refugees, but after waiting a long time for an interview we were not successful. Then we tried to get a visa for entry into Germany but were refused.

We did not have enough money left to pay to be smuggled out of Pakistan. Zafar's job had only been temporary and our money was dwindling away. We had barely enough for food and I had to ration it every day. Zafar's mental state was a constant worry. Our children had no proper schooling and the weather was almost unbearably hot. I did not know what to do to improve our situation other than to submit to the will of God, so I just waited to see what would come next. Perhaps a miracle would change the situation.

One very hot day Yama was playing football outside our small flat when a foreign man approached him and asked in English if he knew where Zafar and his family lived. Yama was able to speak a little English and explained that Zafar was his father. Yama took the man to our flat and Zafar and I were astonished to see Yama accompanied by a tall, handsome, grey-haired Englishman. The man spoke in English and Zafar translated. He introduced himself as Joseph Glasberg and explained he had come to help us get out of Pakistan. 'What?' We all spoke at the same time. Shock! Disbelief! The children showered Zafar with questions. 'How do you know this man? Why is he going to help us? Where is he going to take us? Who gave him our address?'

Zafar could not answer their questions because at that point he did not know the answers himself. He had never met Joe before but soon all became clear. In 1973 Zafar had been awarded a Fulbright scholarship in America, and he was a student in San Francisco for three years. There he formed a large circle of friends from both America and France, and after his return to Afghanistan he had remained in contact with them. Zafar was very good at keeping in touch with this circle of friends, and he wrote to say that he and his family were trying desperately to get out of Pakistan. Two of this friends in particular, Shatsy from the United States and Kamala from France, were so concerned about us that they contacted another member of their circle of friends, Joe, who they thought might be able to help. Joe was English and lived in England, and although he had not known Zafar personally he was so concerned about our situation that he decided to help us get to England. He was a Jew whose parents had escaped from Nazi Germany when he was a baby, and maybe it was this that made him want to help us. He was not a rich man and I wondered how it could be that in this materialistic world a man like Joe would go to all this trouble and expense to travel to Pakistan to help a family of Muslims he had never met before, even though the followers of our two religions had been enemies for centuries. This was a miracle I could hardly believe.

During his stay in Pakistan, Joe was always compassionate and loving to us and was sensitive enough never once to mention his religion while he was with us. To our great relief Joe booked into a hotel. It would have been very difficult to put him up, even if we had been able to make space for him, for fear of the Mujahideen. We were well aware that any association with foreigners would put all our lives in danger. Joe had brought enough money with him to complete all the formalities necessary for us to leave Pakistan. With the help of Zafar, who knew the system in Pakistan, he assured us that the paperwork would be completed and our passports ready, so we would be able to leave for England within two months. We looked at each other in disbelief, remembering what a fortune teller in Rawalpindi had told us just a couple of months previously.

We had been window shopping in the city one mild February day when I spotted a strange sign illustrated with weird drawings which said, 'Come in if you would like to know about your future.' Desperate people do crazy things and I asked Zafar if we could go in, even though I do not really believe in such things as a rule. Zafar laughed at me but I just thought it would be fun. The children were keen too so we knocked on the door and went in. We entered a small, dark room where a man with a long beard sat on a thin mattress. A low table in front of him was covered in books and scattered papers. His skin was dark and he was wrapped in a black shawl. The wall was covered with bizarre signs and posters. He did not look at me, probably because I was a woman, but concentrated on Zafar who explained we had plans to go to America but were having many difficulties along the way and he wondered if we would ever get there. He said this smiling at me almost sarcastically for he obviously thought we were wasting our time.

The fortune teller asked Zafar's name and the names of his parents, and wrote them down. Then he took his hand and studied his palm for about five minutes. After this he opened a book and started to read. When he had finished, he said, 'Your star has been hit by the devil and you have had a rough time lately.' He then told us many things about our past life and we were amazed how true it all was. 'He is a good psychologist', I thought to myself. Then he said, 'You're not going to America, you're going to England soon and you will stay there for the rest of your life.'

We looked at each other and Zafar said, 'We do not plan to go to England.'

'You will be getting help from someone and will be leaving Pakistan very soon', he replied. Then he suddenly stopped talking to Zafar and, avoiding my eyes, he said to me. 'Buy a few pounds of meat, hang one piece of it on your roof to dry and give the rest to the birds. Make a *khatm* in your house.'

Zafar gave him some money and we left the shop. 'Nonsense,' said Zafar. 'We have no friends in England, and our relatives there are not rich enough to help us.' For the rest of the day he teased us, and then we forgot all about it, but I did make a *khatm.* There are many different ways that Muslims can make a *khatm* to pray for help in times of trouble. On this occasion I invited a number of friends to our house and we divided the thirty chapters of the Quran between us, so we all had a section to recite, and together we finished reading the whole Quran in one day.

Zafar and Joe went out every day seeing to our passports. Yama and Parissa were so excited that they told everyone in the neighbourhood, most of whom were Afghan refugees, but no one believed them. Some said that Joe might be a heroin smuggler; others went even further and suggested that Zafar had worked with the Mafia when he was in America. This kind of gossip spread quickly and was a constant worry to us, for it was dangerous to have a bad reputation. Such talk would put us in danger both from the Pakistani police who were always harassing Afghan refugees and from the Mujahideen. Though we never told Joe about what was being said we realized he was a little nervous. He went off to India for a while and when he came back our travel documents were fortunately nearly ready. We finally got our documents with permission to enter Great Britain as visitors under the sponsorship of Joe. Then Joe left for England and three weeks later, on 27 July 1984, we flew from Islamabad to London Heathrow. Without Joe's help we could never have been able to get out of Pakistan, and we were so grateful to him. From this time on until the present day, Joe has remained part of our family, a good brother to me and an uncle to our children.

Chapter Seven
England

I AM A REFUGEE
Spring again
April
The most beautiful season in England
Trees full of blossom, grass and bushes fresh
They remind me of home, a good feeling
Twenty-four long years since in desperation I left my
home country
Shall I see spring in my country again?
Shall I see the silvery water cascading down from
Pagman mountain?
Shall I smell the aroma of fresh bread from our neigh-
bourhood bakery?
Shall I find my home, my dignity?
I AM A REFUGEE

When I was at school I used to hear about Britain
repeatedly from my history teacher. I learnt how
Britain with its mighty empire had failed to conquer
our nation, how our fearless people had defeated the
British on three occasions and how the great Akbar
Khan had led a revolt against the British in the First

England

Anglo Afghan War, killing General MacNaughton and the entire British army of 30,000 soldiers except for one person, a Dr Bryden, who managed to escape. The names of our heroes were engraved on my heart and I was filled with pride and joy in our brave nation. How ironic and strange it seemed to me now, to be in England, in the very heart of Afghanistan's age-old enemy, asking for help and refuge.

We had no problem with the immigration officials at Heathrow airport and were met there by Zafar's brother, Sayed Fazal Rabi, and his sister, Parween, who had arrived in England a few years before us. After such a long separation we had a wonderful reunion, full of tears and joy. Then they drove us to Parween's house where we were to stay. London seemed huge, full of skyscrapers, traffic and people of every race and colour hurrying about their business with no time to look at each other. What a strange world it seemed, like a raging ocean roaring and swallowing up everything that came its way. I felt very uneasy and even more scared than when we lived in Pakistan with all its mosquitoes and flies. I asked myself, 'Why, oh why did we have to come here? What are we going to do with ourselves? Whatever will happen to the children? Will the fear of living here ever leave me?' I felt a strange aching feeling of homelessness and even began to miss the familiarity of Pakistan.

Parween was very kind and helpful and we stayed

with her for three weeks. During this time Joe came to visit us and we visited him in his London flat. Then we moved to my brother-in-law's three-bedroomed flat in Croydon, where he lived with his wife and three children. We spent a further three weeks with him, and he too was very generous and kind and made us all welcome, although it was a squash in the flat for us all. Friends and relatives advised Zafar to apply to the Home Office for political asylum which he immediately did. After a while, we were recognised as asylum seekers and eligible for housing, and it became a routine for Zafar to go to the Council every day in the hope of getting us somewhere to live. They told us that there was no place available in Croydon, but they could offer us accommodation in a hostel in Woking which we readily accepted.

When we got off the train at Woking station we were approached by a tall, beautiful woman called Anthea. She greeted us with a friendly smile and a courteous manner and we immediately felt at ease with her, although we had no idea where she was taking us, what kind of hostel it would be or how long we would have to stay there. After a fifteen-minute drive we stopped in front of a big Victorian house. As we got out of the car and entered our new home, from where we would start to establish our new life in England, I wondered if I would ever again experience a feeling of tranquillity again.

The house was called 'Verrals' and was run by a

charitable organization called the Ockenden Trust. Anthea was the head of the house and she had three additional staff to help her with shopping and visits to the doctor, dentist and optician. The property itself was not in good condition but the richness of the care and understanding we received was quite over-whelming and went a long way towards making adjustment to our new life easier.

The large, three-storey house was already over-crowded with refugees from Vietnam who seemed to be happy in their new environment. There were men and women, young and old, all from different back-grounds and with their own tragic story. Some of the adults had their children with them and there were other children who had come on their own, unaccom-panied by their parents. Each family, no matter the numbers involved was allocated one room. Ours was on the ground floor and had five beds, two smelly bits of carpet and one small wardrobe. The latter did not bother us as we had so few clothes. We had to share the lounge, dining room, kitchen, toilet and bathroom, and while standing in line waiting to use the bathroom was not a pleasant experience, we all did our best not to cause problems for each other. I felt completely lost among so many people and kept asking myself how I was going to cope with all these strangers con-stantly around me. Would there ever be any peace in my life?

The staff were all extremely kind and did their best

to understand our situation and how hard it was to be away from our friends and families. They were sensitive to the little things which made our lives easier. Initially we had to eat with the Vietnamese families in the long, carpetless dining room at a specific time each day, but their food was so different from ours that I could not bring myself to swallow even the rice they cooked. After a few days we asked Anthea if we could cook our own food and she kindly, agreed although the rice and other ingredients she bought for us were very expensive. At 'Verrals' the fridge was always full of good basic food – milk, cheese and vegetables. We were also given fresh fruit every day and we had to assemble after dinner to collect it. This made me feel like a beggar and I always tried to avoid collecting our allocation myself. However, because the staff were so wonderful I soon got over the feelings of isolation and destitution I had when I arrived at the hostel.

As soon as we arrived at 'Verrals' the children were allocated to a local school and in the hostel toys and books were provided for them. Yama and Parissa started school. Within a few weeks Yama, who was now sixteen, was moved to college and although he spoke very little English, he soon made friends and his English improved rapidly. Parissa, who also spoke very little English, was very quiet at school for the first six months, and then amazingly she suddenly started speaking in good English, so in those first six months she must have been taking in a huge amount of language in preparation for the time she felt able to speak.

An English language class was provided for the adults and there I met my teacher, Carole Grace. She was very, very English but although I was from a very different culture and background I felt comfortable being near her and talking to her. Even though she had her own method of teaching, she reminded me of the time when I was a teacher in Afghanistan. She was very firm in class and very friendly out of it. She was not only my teacher but also became a warm-hearted friend who remains very special to me. Her company alone, even when there was not much to say, brought me great comfort. Meeting Carole was the best thing that happened to me at that particular time of need, and to this day I still value every minute of her friendship.

Zafar was completely fluent in English, having studied in America, but although I had learnt a little English at school and university I had never taken it seriously as I never dreamt I would one day be living in England. Learning English was quite a struggle at this stage of my life, and I had to acknowledge that I was a fairly slow learner but it never stopped me trying. When all else failed I communicated with hand gestures and facial expressions which at times were very amusing. However, there were others who struggled even more than me with the language.

There was a Vietnamese man who I guessed was probably illiterate in his own language and had as much difficulty coping with English as he did with the change in lifestyle. He had arrived in England with his two daughters but without his wife. After ten months he was just able to count from one to seven, and every time he passed our room to go upstairs he would hold his youngest girl's hand and try to teach her numbers in English by counting the steps. One, two, three and so on. She would repeat them aloud after him. The problem was that the stairs had ten steps and the poor man was stuck at seven so when he reached the eighth step he would start from one again. The young child soon learned more from Anthea who was very attached to her, but the poor man never got further than seven. I felt very sorry for him.

After eleven months of living at 'Verrals' we were allocated temporary accommodation in a council house in South Norwood in north Croydon. It was wonderful to have a private place of our own with no more sharing of bathroom, toilet and kitchen, but it was not easy to make a home at first. We only had a few blankets and bedclothes the hostel manager kindly gave us. The house was completely empty but the Council gave us £400 and I managed to buy a second-hand cooker, beds, carpets and a few other things. My brother-in-law gave us an old television and Zafar's nephew, visiting us from Germany, offered to climb on the roof to fix the aerial. Zafar and Sulaiman were in our bedroom when suddenly I heard a loud crash and rushed upstairs to see what was going on. Through a fog of dust I saw our guest's long legs hanging from the ceiling and old newspapers falling from the loft on to Zafar's head and shoulders. Sulaiman was screaming, but after our visitor managed to extricate himself from the rafters, everyone calmed down. We put a plaster on Zafar's injured head, had a very good laugh and reported the matter to the Council.

Zafar started to publish a monthly bulletin about Afghanistan, where opposition to the communists continued. I bought an industrial sewing machine so that I would be able to work from home for a factory, although I had never done anything like this before. Parissa and Yama were both getting on well at school and college in Croydon, and I started English classes run by the adult education service in Croydon. We all tried very hard to adapt ourselves to life in our new country. Life began to feel normal once more but this tranquillity did not last long, as Zafar became ill again. One day when I came home from shopping, he was just sitting in the middle of the room. I asked him something and he just looked past me, as if he didn't know me. I spoke to him again, and then I realized that he was completely unable to talk. At first I thought that he was suffering from mental illness again. I rushed to my neighbour for help and although we had not spoken before, she came in quickly. When she saw the state Zafar was in, she immediately called an ambulance and then left me alone to cope.

When the ambulance came I could not explain everything because of the language problem. They took Zafar to Warlingham Psychiatric Hospital, but I felt that nobody took his illness very seriously. He was given some medication which made him sleepy, then after two weeks he was sent to King's College hospital for a heart check-up. There the doctor diagnosed that he was not mentally ill but had had a stroke. We were all relieved that at last he was in the right place and after treatment would be able to come home. I went to visit him every day taking Sulaiman with me on the bus. Then one day I was surprised to find his bed empty. Somehow I managed to ask a nurse where he was and to get the main points of her reply. My surprise turned to alarm when the nurse asked if I had a friend or relative with me. I explained I was alone. 'Is he dead?' I asked. She told me Zafar had had a major heart attack and was on a life support machine. I did not want Sulaiman to see his father in that condition so I went home and came back on my own to visit, when the elder children could look after Sulaiman. Zafar was on that machine for six days and remained in hospital for nearly a month. It was a very long time before he was able to speak at all and he never recovered his speech perfectly. He needed constant care.

England

Unfortunately, because I was so busy looking after Zafar I had to give up my English classes. I no longer had Zafar with his fluent English to rely on. Struggling with language was my greatest problem and visits to the doctor, dentist and optician were a nightmare. I had to practise my limited vocabulary for days and even then, all I could manage to explain was, 'the pain is here' or 'the pain is bad'. Then I would fall silent and feel ridiculous. Going to the supermarket was not so difficult because I did not have to say much, but shopping in the market could be quite awful. Sometimes I waited in long queues, constantly repeating to myself the names of the goods I wanted to buy, and then when it was my turn the words would go straight out of my head. I could see the irritation in some people's faces and feel my own frustration at not being able to express myself. Some people laughed at me, others tried to be helpful and attempted to correct my English by shouting at me as if I was deaf.

Making friends in this situation was out of the question. To socialize you need language, so how could I do that? Another problem was the deep gulf between our cultures. The constant uncertainty about what I should say meant that as often as not I kept silent. I found it strange that casual English conversation so often centred on dogs, cats, drink, food and, most of all, the weather. I heard women in the park talking about their dogs but not their children. Then they would say, 'What a beautiful morning. Isn't it a lovely day?' or 'What lovely sunshine.' Why are they so concerned about the weather? I wondered. There is nothing special about the sun. In Afghanistan we always had the sun and never talked about it. Our conversation would start with family affairs. 'Where do you live?' Have you got any children?'

In July 1986 we were given permanent accommodation in Shrublands, a council estate in the Shirley area of Croydon. The flat we lived in on the ground floor was damp, draughty and very cold without double glazing and central heating, so it was hard for us to keep the bedrooms warm. Parissa developed asthma and had to go to hospital many times. But gradually we all settled down. Parissa, who had moved from her all-girls school in north Croydon to a mixed school nearer our new flat, was doing well in her new school. Yama was able to continue his studies at the same college in Croydon. I started taking Sulaiman to playgroup and it was there that I met some wonderful people who are still my friends today. Satti and Irene, the playgroup leaders, are still my great friends. They made sure I was welcomed into their community and accepted as one of their own. Their understanding and compassion almost made me forget I was a foreigner among them, and the huge gulf I had initially felt between us dissolved in their love and care for me, particularly in the difficult times that were to follow. Only one person rejected me because I was a Muslim and she acted as if I was an infected wound. If only I had had sufficient knowledge of the language at that time I would have explained to her that it is the followers of Islam who are not perfect, not the religion itself, and this could be said of any religion. But apart from her, I had such good friends that I was able to feel part of the Shrublands community and my English improved.

I remember that I met my friend Claire when I was taking Sulaiman to swimming lessons. We started chatting to each other at the swimming pool as we sat watching our children, and, although my English was not very good, I managed to make myself understood. I was really touched when she invited me to tea because I always thought English people only asked those they knew well to their houses. Here was someone I hardly knew who was willing to extend the hand of friendship to me. We soon became firm friends.

In 1989 the Soviet Union pulled out of Afghanistan, and Zafar and I seriously considered going home, but finally decided against it as we felt that the political situation was so unstable that it would be foolish to endanger our lives and those of our children. Sadly, it did not take us long to realise that the holy war waged against the invading Russians for honour and principle had changed to a pointless civil war between warring factions. At the same time as this civil war was being fought, there was a growth in the influence of Islamic fundamentalism that we had seen in the Pakistan refugee camps, under the Mujahideen.

We were particularly alarmed at the growth in the power of the Taliban. The Taliban preached a very strict and extreme form of Islam, where women had no freedom at all and where simple pleasures like kite flying were banned. Muslims believe in the idea of a holy war of *jihad* if the cause is just, and Zafar and I felt it was justified to fight to overthrow the Russians. But the Taliban took the concept of *jihad* to the extreme and introduced a reign of terror against anyone who did not accept their dogma. The Afghanistan where Zafar and I had belonged in the past was a moderate Muslim country, and we did not feel we could fit into a country where extremism was becoming a powerful force. For us *jihad* has a deeper meaning which is the sincere effort to live according to the highest teaching of the Muslim faith.

In January 1992 we had a very happy occasion, when Yama got married to Surrita. Surrita's father was Indian and her mother English. Surrita was brought up a Hindu and we were Muslim, and because of these differences at first both families found the relationship difficult to accept. However, soon Surrita's family came to like Yama and to accept him as son-in-law. Surrita was very young, shy and quiet and at first she found it hard to communicate with me. My English was very poor and also adjusting to another culture was not easy for both of us, but although it was difficult at the beginning, later we managed to get on well. She became a big part of our family.

Then in August 1992 a bitter tragedy occurred in my family which we will never get over. At four o'clock one morning I had a call from Parissa, who had been at a party at my sister-in-law's flat with Zafar. She told me something terrible had happened. I immediately thought Zafar had had another heart attack but the news concerned Ruhullah, Zafar's nephew. Ruhullah was twenty-four years old, very talented, gentle, peace-loving and very handsome. He was planning to become a doctor. He had been badly beaten up by a gang of fourteen racists, armed with makeshift clubs and iron bars just outside his family's flat, and was now in hospital. My knees turned to water and I collapsed on the floor. Then I rushed over to the flat in the Thornton Heath area of Croydon and heard that Ruhullah had had a four-hour operation on his head at the specialist Atkinson Morley Hospital, but it was not successful. His life support machine was switched off after four days and he died at the hospital on 2 August. That day we were left with a lifetime of grieving. A light went out and a good life was wasted for nothing. Perhaps it was his destiny to be dragged all the way from war-torn Afghanistan only to die in a pool of blood on the streets of a so-called civilized country.

The police investigated the murder and there was widespread coverage of the story in the newspapers and on television. The police were kind, sensitive and helpful to us. We received many letters of sympathy, cards and flowers from people all over the country. Every morning for nearly three weeks, flowers were left at the place where Ruhullah was attacked. God knows where we would have been without this support and compassion. We learnt that humanity had not died and of course it never will, completely. We may sometimes feel alone but there are many people who do care and are fighting against injustice in the world.

Ruhullah had been attacked by a group of fourteen teenagers, but just three of them were jailed and the rest walked free. Four years later we heard that one of the boys had been released early from prison, according to the law, and I came to realize that sadly the law does not necessarily mean justice. After the murder, everyone in our extended family grieved in their own way. Although we all tried to keep our pain to ourselves, the once cheerful atmosphere changed to one of tension and strain. Zafar was profoundly affected by the murder. He withdrew into himself and just sat watching television or occasionally went for a walk. Parissa's asthma worsened and she went through a long and deep depression. I believe she still suffers today as a result of what happened. Yama and Surrita, who had recently got married, had a shadow hanging over their new life together. Sulaiman was scared to go to sleep. My husband's nephew, Haron, needed counselling and Ruhullah's mother suffered a heart attack. Still further sadness was to follow.

In February 1993 Zafar had another stroke. He lost his balance and fell, hitting his head as he did so. Within a very few minutes he was in a coma which was to last a month. He was in Bromley Hospital for seven further months and seeing him lying between those white sheets all that time, unable to move or speak, became an agonizing nightmare for me and my family. I used to go in every morning and stay there till lunch time, and the children visited after school. I was so grateful to my friends who supported me at the time, especially Karin and Trevor Allen. Trevor used to drive me to the hospital and wait to take me home afterwards, which was such a help.

At first Zafar could not eat but after a month I was able to feed him with a teaspoon. One morning, I went earlier than usual to find there were no nurses on the ward. I found Zafar lying face down at the edge of the bed. His blanket had fallen off and he was completely naked. He was trying to change his position, struggling with one hand. For a second I stood there horrified, then I went straight to the nurses' station and they quickly made him more comfortable, but I felt his humiliation and wondered how long he had lain like that.

In those long hours as I sat next to Zafar and held

his hand my memories dragged me back into the past, to our former life in Afghanistan. I thought of our home there when we were first married, the huge bungalow with twelve rooms, the large, fertile piece of land with the vineyard and fruit trees, and how my mother-in-law as head of the household had organized everything for us. There were three married sons with their wives and children, and three unmarried sons and daughters living there. As we were all busy working and studying, she hired servants who lived in a separate compound. I remembered how one evening after dinner everyone had gone to their rooms but Zafar had disappeared. Suddenly we heard a loud noise and laughter coming from the big hall. We found Zafar leading a procession of servants carrying banners and marching along the corridor shouting, 'Our wages are not enough, we want more!' The servants and their children were shouting after him and everyone was laughing and enjoying themselves. This demonstration ended happily, for my mother-in-law was in a good mood and promised to raise the servants' wages from the following month. It was so typical of Zafar to act like this, and the servants loved him as he was always on their side.

In those lingering months at his bedside I remembered happier days. I recalled the time when Zafar had asked me to go to Kabul airport with him because one of his friends was arriving from abroad after a

Zafar and I at Yama and Surrita's wedding

long time away. He wanted us to welcome him home. The next day we drove to the airport. I was wearing my casual clothes and my little son, Yama, was with me. When we got to the airport Zafar dismissed the chauffeur, who I was expecting would drive us back. I found it odd and it was then I realized that nobody was coming from abroad. Instead Zafar told me we were to go to Russia and then on to America for a holiday to celebrate our wedding anniversary. It was the nicest surprise and the best present I could have had. That was the sort of man Zafar was.

On another occasion, he came home with two tickets for his sister and I to go to the movies. We had a lovely day out seeing the film and window shopping. At the end of the day, my sister-in-law suggested we visit a friend of hers, someone I did not know. She stopped the car outside an apartment and I saw my son, Yama, who was then about four years old. He was with his maid Sanobar and I thought this was very odd because they were not supposed to go out without my permission. I hurried towards them to find out what they were doing there, but when Sanobar saw me she picked up Yama and ran towards the building. Before I could reach them they were inside and when I rang the bell Sanobar opened the door with a lovely smile on her face. Before I had time to question her, Zafar came out of a room and said, 'Welcome to your flat, it is all yours.' The flat was decorated just right for my taste with everything brand new. I was so happy, because I was finding it really difficult living in an extended family and had been longing for the privacy of my own place. Later on I found out that my sister-in-law had been in on the secret and had been helping Zafar for the last few months to get the flat ready for me.

I recalled that cold, autumn evening when he came home with two bags of grapes. It surprised me because he was not the sort of man to bring food home, or help me with the shopping. I thought it was a good sign. My maid Leila took the grapes to wash, but after a short while she came back and whispered in my ear that the grapes were rotten. She asked me to see for myself and she was right, they were rotten. I asked Zafar why he had wasted money on such bad grapes. He replied, 'Don't exaggerate, they are not very bad. Keep them for me and I will eat them.' Leila washed some of the grapes and threw the rest away. I made fun of Zafar and told everyone about it and he was laughing too. Later, he told me the real reason he had bought the grapes. He had seen an old man shivering with cold, trying to sell the grapes from a broken trolley, but no one was buying them because they were bad. Zafar felt sorry for the old man and bought the lot. When I asked him why he had not just given the man money instead of buying the rotten fruit, he replied, 'Because I was sure the poor man would not go home until he had sold his grapes.'

One day as I sat thinking, the nurse brought me back from the past to the dreadful reality of seeing my husband in that helpless state. When she gave him his medicine, he could not swallow and began to choke. After a long while, he began to breathe normally and drifted off to sleep. For the only time in my life I prayed, 'Dear God, please forgive him and take him from me. Let him die in peace.' Zafar died in 1993 at the age of fifty two. He was buried on his birthday, 19 September. Life does not seem the same without him and I miss him dreadfully, despite his many faults and weaknesses.

Zafar's death created for me such a terrible feeling of hopelessness, that I thought my heart would burst.

In many ways he had not been an ideal husband, and had developed a bachelor-type of lifestyle since his early teens. Despite a great understanding of politics, poetry, English and mathematics, he was very disorganized and erratic. He was never able to function as a family man and take the burden off my shoulders as I would have liked. He always left me to take full responsibility for the children and somehow I always felt like a single parent. Over the last thirteen years he had lost mental stability and seemed to change into a different person. One way or another, my life had revolved round prison, mental institutions and hospitals. He knew he was often to blame for things that caused trouble in our relationship but he loved me and the children very much. This had bound us together whatever happened. He always knew that when he was in trouble I would stand by him and get him out.

Despite his faults, he had so many good qualities when he was well, a kind and generous nature, and he was always compassionate to the poor and needy. He did not love money for itself, but used his money for those who he thought might need it. In Afghanistan there was a big gulf between the rich and the poor but Zafar was unusual in that he tried to break down these divisions. He would help our servants to get better working conditions, and would help them in other ways and even eat with them, while everybody else in the family kept their distance from them according to Afghan custom. He valued friendship deeply and had a great capacity for making and keeping friends, including many from overseas. He believed in the human race without regard to colour or power.

Now he was gone. In my mind I always re-lived our escape from Afghanistan, our harsh life in Pakistan, living in exile in England, like a sad film. It made me a prisoner of the past. When Zafar died, all the years of hoping and praying and waiting to go back to where I belonged, to friends and relatives with whom I have common memories, were suddenly buried with his body.

Chapter Eight
Where do I belong?

I have been shaped and framed by a black chaderi
I am an invisible creature
Deprived of the right of education
They insulted my intelligence
They invaded my freedom
They committed crimes and put me in prison
I am a prisoner of men's cruelty and ignorance
I am a chained woman with blindfolded eyes
My right is at the mercy of my uncle and my younger
brother
My identity is stolen from me
But I cannot carry this burden on my shoulders
I shall break the chain
I shall escape from the cage
I shall get my dignity back
Because life without dignity is worthless

Zafar's death left me with deep fear, anger and much sorrow. I felt like a tired traveller confronted by a stone wall of silence and loneliness. I was left alone with Sulaiman who was just nine years old. Yama, who was working for an insurance company, and his

153

Where do I belong?

Parissa and I at her graduation in 1999

wife had their own flat in north Croydon. They had their own lives to lead. Parissa left home a year after Zafar died. After leaving sixth-form college she worked for a short time and then went to London University. I was pleased that my two eldest children were making a success of their lives in England and living independently, but I missed them greatly. With only Sulaiman at home with me, I had to take on the full burden of dealing with all the practical problems of everyday life with my limited English as well as my own emotions.

I was very depressed at the time and Sulaiman was missing his father very much. He was at the local primary school and one of the teachers, Janis Say, realised what a difficult time it was for him and offered to give him guitar lessons after school. Sulaiman was really keen to learn the guitar and it certainly helped to take this mind off his problems. I was very grateful to Janis, who has remained a good friend.

Dealing with my paper work was a major problem. Every morning when the postman delivered an official letter from the council or anywhere else, it was a nightmare for me. I had to take the letter to the Shrublands Advice Centre to ask for help. The advice worker was a lay Minister for the Shrublands Christian Fellowship called Graham Woolgar. He had trained as a social worker and he was a wonderful support, always ready to help with all my paperwork. I felt like a full-time client for him, and as this went on I

Where do I belong?

Sulaiman and I at his graduation in 2005

realised I had to learn English to stop being so dependent. I joined an English class again near our flat on the council estate. We were only four students in the class and luckily had two volunteer teachers. By this time I knew a little English and enjoyed the class very much.

However, I wanted to get on faster and did not like reading simple children's books. I wanted to read books at my own level and was frustrated that it was still impossible, so every day after I dropped my son at his school and finished my two-hour class I went to Croydon Library and spent hours among the books. I did not know what I was looking for but enjoyed the calmness of the atmosphere. One day I found a book called *Gone with the Wind* which I had read long ago in Dari translation when I was a teenager. It was my favourite book at that time and it had a profound effect on me. I borrowed the book and started reading it at home with the help of a dictionary. I knew the story already which helped, but it took me eight or nine months to finish the whole book. I just understood about 30 per cent but that was an achievement, and marked the point when my English really began to improve. My next project was *Les Miserables* by Victor Hugo, another challenging book which I managed to complete. After that Croydon library was my second home.

I was still feeling depressed and I got a lot of help from my GP, Doctor Clark, who always had time to listen to my problems. I felt I needed to move house, as Shrublands reminded me of Zafar and all the sadness of his death. Dr Clark helped me to apply to be housed in a different area, and I was allocated a small house in South Croydon. It was in a good area, with a garden, and I threw myself into making it into a real home for Sulaiman and myself. Slowly I began to come to terms with my grief.

Now that I was more confident about my English, I joined a bilingual counselling course at Thornton Heath Adult Education Centre, because I wanted to use my language skills to support others from Afghanistan. In fact, I needed counselling myself at this stage, and the course helped me to develop skills which I could apply to both my own situation and that of others. As part of the course, the teacher gave us homework and asked us to write whatever we felt. This prompted me to start thinking about my own story and the idea of writing a book shaped in my mind, as a way of easing the pain that accumulated in my heart all these years.

When the bilingual counselling course came to an end the group had the idea of setting up a voluntary organization offering support to refugees and others with English as their second language. With support from our teacher, we founded Helppoint, a bilingual advice service which operated from an office at Thornton Heath Adult Education Centre. We received an award as outstanding adult learners from the

National Institute of Adult and Continuing Education, and we even managed to get some funding to pay some Helppoint staff.

I worked for Helppoint, and after completing a community interpreting course, I started to work as a freelance interpreter. I also did voluntary work for another organisation, Refugee Project Croydon, advising and supporting other refugees. Refugees are the most vulnerable people on earth, and in my work I shared their miseries. Many are highly qualified – doctors, engineers, teachers, writers and professors who spent all their young lives studying and held important positions in their own countries. Now they are scattered all over the world, working in restaurants, cleaning swimming pools, or, if they are lucky, driving taxis. They have to be content with being second-class citizens in a foreign country.

I was the interpreter for two teenage brothers who came from Afghanistan. They had suffered great hardship on their way to England. They told me that the smuggler took them to Russia and told them that it was London and he then disappeared. In Moscow they went underground for a whole year, working here and there to survive, bribing the Russian police. They worked hard, saved some money and found another smuggler who arranged for them to travel to England. They walked through woods for many nights and slept during the days. Then they were passed on to a chain of different smugglers. At one point they travelled in a lorry, which was boarded into two separate areas, upper and lower. The women and children were squashed into the upper area while the older boys and men were down below. None of them could stand up as there was no room. As they were not allowed out at all until they reached their destination, the women and children's urine leaked through the boards onto to the heads of the men and people underneath. The boys were laughing when they told me their story, but I sensed the tragedy behind their laughter.

When they reached London they heard that their father had been killed in the civil war and left a large family. In London one of the boys fell ill. When I met him, he was severely depressed and even thought I was his mother. Seeing him took me back to the time in my life when Zafar was locked up in a mental institution. Now the boy is out of hospital but on medication. His brother is a taxi driver, with little English, and also suffering from depression. He has to support a large family, who are thousands of miles away. This is just one example of what refugees have to deal with. When I was dealing with cases like this, it really affected me, especially as I knew from my own experience what it was like to be a refugee.

I enjoyed working as an interpreter but it is very difficult to get full-time work. Most interpreters are employed part-time, as the need arises. I was being paid well one month, but then had nothing the next

and this was something Croydon Council could not cope with. They assumed that I was earning much more than I was and stopped the rent for my home. I was really frightened that Sulaiman and I would become homeless. I went to the Housing Benefit Agency many times, but nobody would listen to me. Then I was horrified to receive a letter summoning me to court. Luckily Bob Dorey, the husband of my good friend Irene from playgroup days, paid the out-standing rent for me and then spent many weeks sorting out the problem. Finally, he got his money back. In the end I was forced to give up paid work, as I could not risk losing my home. I felt there was something wrong with a government system that did not encourage people to earn their own living.

I continued working voluntarily with refugees, pleased that now I felt more confident myself about leading an independent life in England, I was able to make a real contribution towards supporting the very difficult transition that other refugees have to make to adapt to life in a new country. The older generation of Afghans struggle with culture, language and religion. The younger generation know little about their country of origin; they are confused, lost and hurt and have to carry the heavy weight of two cultures on their young shoulders. Most are affected by European social life and reject Afghan social values, back-ground and customs. This can lead to a breakdown in communication between parents and their children.

Where do I belong?

Some youngsters adopt the negative part of British culture, drinking heavily and going wild. This kind of behaviour creates alarm, fear, shame and heartache to those who are brought up in a very conservative way so they get more and more strict with their children and try to keep them from integrating into their new country. They completely isolate themselves, ignorant of the outside world, of the English language and their rights. They do not even know their neighbours. There are some men who work and socialize freely outside their community, but are not happy for their wives and female relatives to mix with English people or lead independent lives.

Many Afghan women are reluctant to even attempt to adapt to their new Western surroundings without their husband's permission. They focus instead on being the obedient wives their husbands demand them to be. In terms of the English language they completely depend on their husbands and children; they are helpless, lonely and isolated. Some women attempt to integrate into their new country, and go through a long battle with their husbands, ending in divorce. The rate of divorce among Afghan refugees in the UK and United States is very high, much higher than in Afghanistan. Unfortunately the word 'freedom' is misunderstood by some Afghan men. In their eyes it means loose women, while what Afghan women want is equality in education, jobs and basic human rights.

Where do I belong?

I had always led an independent life as a woman in Afghanistan. At the time when I was at school and university, the education of women was encouraged, and the government supported the emancipation of women, although many people did not agree with this. After my marriage, Zafar always encouraged me to earn my own living. He was quite unusual among Afghan men in his liberal attitudes towards women, and he never tried to stop me from doing anything. It is not commonly known in the West that in Afghanistan the first steps towards the emancipation of women were taken in 1921 by King Amanullah Khan who was eager to modernize the country, though he tried to move too fast and there was a lot of opposition to his policies. His own wife, Queen Soraya, did not wear the veil in public. He opened schools for girls and sent graduate students abroad for higher education. After his reign, the independence of women which had taken a step forward went backwards for three decades until in1959, when I was twelve years old, women were no longer required to wear the veil. The clerics from Kandahar province rebelled but the government was fully prepared and did not back down. In 1964 women were granted equal rights under the law. In the 1960s and 1970s women were admitted to university, although there had been all-women colleges since 1946. At my time at Kabul University there were almost as many girls as boys, and women were involved in all professions including medicine, law, banking and media. At that time, even in the most underdeveloped parts of the country, women knew that they were an important part of their society.

I remember the day when my father decided to buy me a *chaderi.* In Afghanistan the *chaderi* was invented in the late 19th century by the royal family who wanted to be distinguished from the rest of the country, and also to have their privacy respected. It was a sign of pride and wealth to cover the face and body completely with only a small window-like piece of embroidery in front of the eyes to see through. Slowly through the years it became part of our culture, and was worn especially in the big cities, even though covering the face has no basis in the Quran. My father thought I was of the age to attract undesirable attention, so he bought me a *chaderi* and at first I felt thrilled with the excitement of looking grown-up wearing it. Then, after the equal rights legislation in 1964, girls no longer had to cover themselves, and I remember the feelings, first of guilt and then of freedom, as I walked out in the streets uncovered. My father was not happy about it but he could not do anything against the government's decision.

During the civil war between the different factions of the Mujahideen, the status of women was lowered once again. Then in 1996, when the Taliban came to power and imposed their harsh, brutal laws, women seemed to lose their rights completely. The Taliban closed down girls' schools, fired women teachers, banned women from working and going to university. They even forced people to paint their house windows black so that the women inside could not be seen from outside. Lipstick and nail polish were out of the question. The face and body had to be completely covered with a *chaderi*, and any woman who showed her ankle or wrist was beaten. Women were not even allowed to wear shoes that made a noise, and white shoes were banned in case they attracted men's attention. Male doctors were not allowed to see female patients.

I am sure that there is no basis in the Quran for denying women basic human rights. The Prophet Mohammed permitted women to be active outside the home. Among his own wives, Aisha was active in politics and Khadija was a business woman. In fact Khadija proposed to Prophet Mohammed, while today a woman proposing to a man would be unthinkable. The Taliban were religious fanatics who had little understanding of Islam, unaware of the equality which has existed in Muslim history.

I met a young couple who had escaped from Afghanistan under the Taliban through the Refugee Project where I worked. The man told me that he had been with a group of people travelling by coach to Kabul. It was afternoon prayer time and the bus stopped for all the passengers to pray. Then they started the journey again. After fifteen minutes they reached a checkpoint and were stopped by soldiers. After searching them, one of the soldiers ordered them to do their prayers. They explained that they had just prayed. The soldier did not believe them and forced them to do it again. Being scared, they obeyed. When they had finished, a very fragile old man who took the soldier's behaviour as an insult to his faith, turned his face from the direction of Mecca and in indignation prayed and bowed to the soldier. When asked the reason, he replied 'I had finished my prayer to my own God a while ago but this one is for you, because you are a god too, in this lawless country.' The soldier began to beat the man with his gun, and although the other passengers tried to stop him it was too late. The older man collapsed and if it had not been for the other passengers who put him on the bus and did their best to care for him he would have been left to die.

I was horrified to hear the terrible stories from Afghanistan under the Taliban and was grateful that the children and I were able to make our lives in Britain. Since 1989 we had been granted Indefinite Leave to Remain, which meant we had a permanent right to stay in Britain. We had a travel document which meant we could travel abroad but not to Afghanistan. We knew we could also apply for British citizenship with all the benefits of a British passport. We felt safe in Britain.

I felt very proud when the first edition of my book

was published in 2000. I was asked to speak about my experiences in schools and at conferences. I also spoke to volunteers training to teach English about what it is like to be a refugee and to learn a new language as an adult. I became great friends with the volunteer organiser Joy Burns. I also became involved in more charity work. I felt honoured when I was asked to become a trustee for the Ruth Hayman Trust, a charity that raises money to support the education of refugees and others who have English as a second language. Through this charity work I made many good friends, including Mary Simpson who worked with me to produce this second edition of my book.

Then on 11 September 2001, I was walking along Croydon High Street, when suddenly I was attracted to a crowd of people watching something on TV in the window of a shop. A woman was screaming and someone else was throwing himself out of a building, and tower blocks were crumbling. I realized some-thing very serious had happened, but I never thought it related to my country Afghanistan.

Later on it became very obvious that it had every-thing to do with my poor country, as the terrorists who blew up the Twin Towers were linked with Afghanistan and the Taliban regime and, in the minds of many people, all Afghans were implicated. For the first few weeks after the bombing, I hardly went out and was scared for my son's life at school. Every morning I had to remind him not to mention that he was from

Where do I belong?

Afghanistan. The tragedy affected many Afghan families and dramatically changed some lifestyles and views forever. One man told me how after 9/11 he was very self- conscious about his beard; he shaved it off but was uncomfortable about his Islamic name. Others turned against America, saying that civilians have been killed in Palestine, Afghanistan and Iraq daily for years and they were glad that America now felt their pain for once. Then the Americans and their allies started to bomb Afghanistan, the Taliban were overthrown, and there was war again. My poor nation ended up again as the victim of all the misguided policies of the last twenty five years.

After the fall of Taliban in 2002 and the establishment of the new government under President Hamid Karzai, I felt that at last it was safe for me to visit Afghanistan, after twenty-two years in exile. I was both excited and frightened. The prospect of going back to a land I had not seen in over twenty years which had undergone such pain and anguish seemed daunting. I was really glad that my daughter Parissa was coming with me. She had always been an adventurous traveller, ever since our journey over the mountains to Pakistan, and she was very keen to see the country of her birth. By now we both had British passports which would enable us to enter Afghanistan freely.

We travelled on a luxurious British airways flight

from London to Dubai. Then we changed out of our Western clothes and put on traditional Afghan dress before boarding another plane heading for Afghanistan. We were the only females on the plane. Looking down as we were about to land, I saw a breathtaking view of the wild mountains and was overcome by the harsh beauty of the landscape that I had missed for so long. From the distance all you could see was nature, not the ruins that lay beneath. My heart began to beat with excitement. I felt I was in a dream-like state. At last we landed at Kabul Airport and, with my emotions running high, I felt like crying and kissing the ground.

But the picture before me came as a shock because it was quite different from the one I had carried in my head for so long. I looked around and all I saw was a large piece of grey, bone-dry land, punctuated everywhere with bits of Russian tanks and the rusting remains of cars and lorries. No trees, no greenery, no flowers. Everything, even the people, seemed covered in grey dirt or dust. The land was ruined.

We entered the dilapidated airport building. There did not appear to be any rules or regulations about going through the customs. We could not even tell who was an official and who was not. We joined the queue where incoming passengers appeared to be checked. Suddenly a woman appeared by our side, pulled us out from the queue and took our passports before disappearing into a small cabinet. We panicked. We did not have Afghan passports and were terrified at losing our British ones. But the woman returned, gave back our passports, welcomed us and let us go. I had no idea why she saved us from the queue. Perhaps she expected to receive some kind of reward, or maybe she was just a kind person. Later on, when we learned how those who help passengers to queue-jump usually demand money, I felt bad for not having given the woman any. Three men rushed towards us to help us with our luggage. They were fighting over who should have the privilege and, although the amount we were prepared to give them did not warrant three men, we hired them all so as not to create any more tension.

We passed through the airport entrance gate and there waiting for us was my eldest brother, Sayed Shah, and his daughter. It was such an emotional moment, seeing him after so long. He seemed to me to be a hundred years old. Two little boys followed us as we walked towards a taxi, begging for change. What I saw on the way to my brother's house was startling. I expected the country to be poverty-stricken, but not to this extent. People were covered in dust and the roads were a mess. The city of Kabul lay between clouds of dust. No traffic lights, no zebra crossing, no traffic police. There were old men lying on the streets, some with no arms, some with no legs, begging for money. I felt as if I was watching a horror film set in the Stone Age. We arrived at my brother's tiny house with its muddy front garden, home to thirteen people and badly in need of repair.

Seeing my brother's family was something I had dreamed about for so long, and was so moving that I am unable to fully describe it. It was wonderful to be reunited again. After the fall of the Taliban, my brother and his family, who had lived in exile in Pakistan for ten years, returned to their home and were trying hard to adjust to the harsh reality of living conditions in Afghanistan today. They were nevertheless happy to be back, because they were free from the hatred heaped on them by the Pakistani police, who gave refugees such a hard time, demanding money from time to time for no reason. If they were refused money, the police then made up false accusations against the Afghan refugees and they could end up in prison.

The electricity in Kabul was very limited. People had only about three hours of use every alternate evening and there was no electricity available during the day at all. Richer families might be lucky enough to buy a generator and create their own power, but the rest of the population had to make do. My brother's family was overjoyed that I bought them a generator for 6,000 Afghani – equal to £60. Most houses did not have running water. Being able to take a shower with hot water is for most a luxurious dream. What really stunned me was how people managed to get about in Kabul. Pedestrians and cars, cyclists, children, lorries, animals and beggars all shared the same traffic lanes. In some better areas, police were deployed as traffic marshals who tried their best, in vain, to bring some sort of order to the streets. Cars wildly sped right past them. The taxi drivers were the craziest, driving at a suicidal speed you never find anywhere else in the world. I doubt if many of them had driving licences. Children played in the streets with whatever interesting scraps of rubbish they could find, ending up burning them for fun and for warmth, and oddly enough this actually helped to rid the streets of germ-infested litter.

Many things were very difficult for me to adapt to. People in Kabul had no access to sanitary facilities and there was no sewage system in place so people had to use holes they dug in the ground themselves. Every now and then a man came along with a donkey to collect everyone's waste. Children in Kabul were not children any more. They were small adults, robbed of their childhood, working hard alongside adults just to survive. They would walk long distances just to fetch water while also looking after their younger siblings while their parents would be off somewhere else working for a little money. Some of the children, as young as eight or nine, worked as shop assistants in bakeries or in butcher's shops. Those not lucky enough to have jobs walked the streets begging for money. I saw a little girl in the middle of a traffic jam selling two pieces of toilet

Young boy carrying water in Kabul

tissues. Life was such a struggle for those children who truly had to fight to survive. There were thousands of children in the streets of Kabul who were living in such harsh conditions and sleeping rough. I kept asking myself what happened to all the aid that went to Afghanistan. It could have saved those children if nothing else.

The only hope I saw was provided by the Khorasan Organization founded in 1999 in Pakistan, by a brave Afghan lady called Seema Ghani who devoted herself to providing a home for homeless children. The Khorasan House recently moved to Afghanistan after

Where do I belong?

Visiting children at the Khorasan orphanage

the fall of the Taliban. I visited the orphanage in Kabul and it was wonderful to see how these children now have a real home, an education and hope for the future. What touched me most was the way the children looked upon Seema as a real mother. They were climbing all over her, tugging at her dress, giving her big hugs – showing real love. However, this small organization's good work is a drop in the ocean when you look at the poverty that runs rampant across the whole of Afghanistan.

The most upsetting thing I came across in Afghanistan was the state of the country's government.

There was a great sense of mismanagement, poor communication, rivalry, distrust and tribalism in all government offices. The amount of bribery and corruption used to make things happen was sky high. Every office you entered, they would ask you to give them a little extra money for their services.

After the bombing of Afghanistan, people expected America to get fully involved with the reconstruction of the country and not just hunting down the Taliban. All I saw were some high-rise buildings, which belonged to rich people, either foreigners or warlords whom nobody dared ask how and where they got their money from. High rise buildings were springing up in Vazeer Akbar Khan, a posh area in Kabul, while the rest of the country was in a shambles. I was left wondering again where all the foreign aid had gone as I could not see anything more than a few newly asphalted streets.

I was also disappointed to find that the position of women had not really changed since the overthrow of the Taliban. They were just as far from achieving equality with men as they ever were. There were a select few who had been picked to work in offices simply as a front to give the impression that things were changing. However, the majority of Afghan women had not been given the opportunity to play a real part in the reconstruction of their country, and did not have anything like the independence I had enjoyed both as a student and teacher. Afghanistan is a man-made society and the superiority of males is still made very clear in households and outside. Women are still under the domination of their husbands, brothers and fathers. Men often feel threatened by a strong woman and refuse to work under female management.

While it was very sad to see the conditions in Afghanistan, we had a wonderful reception from my brother and his family and experienced how people can make a good life with so little. As guests we were treated like royalty. We ate delicious fresh food, which tasted better to me than what we buy in English supermarkets. Because most people are too poor to have a fridge or freezer, they go out shopping every day so food is really fresh and nothing is processed. In the evenings, many people would call at the house, and we ended up chatting and singing. In Afghanistan there is no need to make an appointment to visit friends as in England; people drop in all the time. Parissa loved it, especially playing with the young children. As a fluent Dari speaker, she was able to join in all the chatting, singing and games of cards.

However, I felt very much a visitor in my own country, which had changed so much from the land I knew. Apart from my brother and his family I could not find a face I knew from the old days. I realized how hard life was for most Afghans and that there was no longer a place for me to live permanently in Afghanistan. I had changed during my twenty-two years of exile, and I realized how difficult I would find it to live under the restrictions many women face.

So now I recognize that Britain is my second home and the home of my children. As a British citizen, I feel grateful for all the help I have received from the government and from British people. I have been treated well. This is a just, lawful and democratic country, and I appreciate the freedom of speech and human rights. Here you are generally known for what you are and not for who your father is or how much money you have. There is no doubt that sometimes I feel out of place in Britain, but I felt equally out of place when I went back to Afghanistan. Perhaps that is the fate of the first generation refugee, to feel displaced, torn between two countries.

My story is a simple cry for myself and my people who died, suffered, lost their children, became disabled, were widowed and became refugees. I hope I have made it clear how we Afghans suffered from a series of terrible political events – war with Russia and civil war between different factions of the Mujahideen leading to the creation of the Taliban – and how this led to the abandonment of human rights, including the rights of women. I would like this story to be my legacy to my dearest children. Because of my eventful life I was not able to offer you stability when you were young, but I hope in writing this I will help you to know your own country through my love for it. And I convey my message to you that, no matter what the future may bring, you must stay close together as a family and learn to be proud of your roots as I am always.